AIVR 2025

The Second International Conference on Artificial Intelligence and Immersive Virtual Reality

April 6 - 10, 2025

Valencia, Spain

AIVR 2025 Editors

Jérôme Dinet, Université de Lorraine, France
Zahra Moussavi, University of Manitoba, Canada

Printed from e-media with permission by:

Curran Associates, Inc.
57 Morehouse Lane
Red Hook, NY 12571

Some format issues inherent in the e-media version may also appear in this print version.

International Academy, Research, and Industry Association (IARIA)
412 Derby Way
Wilmington, DE 19810

Phone: (408) 893-6407
Fax: (408) 527-6351

petre@iaria.org

Additional copies of this publication are available from:

Curran Associates, Inc.
57 Morehouse Lane
Red Hook, NY 12571 USA
Phone: 845-758-0400
Fax: 845-758-2633
Email: curran@proceedings.com
Web: www.proceedings.com

Table of Contents

Designing a Naturalistic and Interactive VR Museum Environment With a Realistic Avatar as a Guide for Cognitive Treatment of the Elderly 1
Amir Bani Saeed and Zahra Moussavi

Non-Immersive Virtual Reality as a Safer Alternative for Cognitive Training in Older Adults: Investigating the Effect of Age on Cybersickness 3
Rashmita Chatterjee and Zahra Moussavi

Acceptability of an AI-Powered Wearable Ring Sensor for Upper Body Mobility in Individuals with Cognitive Impairment: A Pilot Stud 5
Holly Shannon, Asma Seraj Pour Shooshtarib, Logan Young, Makara Rolle, Jennifer O'Neil, Jose Carlos Tatmatsu-Rocha, Dahlia Kairy, Olga Theou, Zahra Moussavi, Ke Peng, and Mirella Veras

Extended Reality (XR) vs. Virtual Reality (VR) for Artificial Intelligence (AI)-Driven Balance Improvement in Older Adults 8
Mirella Veras, Asma Seraj Pour Shooshtarib, Zahra Moussavi, and Ke Peng

Employing Optical Brain Imaging for Real-Time Assessment of Brain Functions During Immersive Virtual Reality: Harnessing Potential for Neurorehabilitation 11
Asma Seraj Pour Shooshtari, Mirella Veras, Ali Kassab, Daniel Alejandro Galindo Lazo, Frederic Lesage, Dang Khoa Nguyen, Zahra Moussavi, and Ke Peng

Towards Personalized Mobility Assessment and Rehabilitation: A User Centered Designed VR/XR-Based Solution for Older Adults 15
Yann Morere, Jerome Dinet, Fabien Clanche, Thierry Bastogne, Matthieu Casteran, Lucas Detto, Matthieu Burtin, Frederic Bousefsaf, and Kaoutar El Ghabi

Enhancing the Utilization of Artificial Intelligence and Social Robots in Specialized Units for Children with Autism 25
Marie Rychalski, Armand Manukyan, and Jerome Dinet

Ergonomic Challenges and Benefits of Enhanced Cultural Application with Augmented Reality for People with Autistic Spectrum Disorder 31
Armand Manukyan, Antoine Pollet, Stephanie Claudel, Jerome Dinet, and Laurent Dupont

The Effects of Virtualization on Connectedness, Presence, and Immersion: A Mixed-Methods Comparison of Real, Mixed, and Virtual Environments 38
Niklas Groffner

Intergenerational Codesign of Immersive Technology for a Heritage Site and Underwater VR Experience 48
Marius Nicolae Varga, Oksana Hagen, Rory Baxter, Alejandro Veliz Reyes, Ray B. Jones, Amir Aly, Dena Bazazian, and Swen Gaudl

Addressing the Symbol Grounding Problem in VR 56
Muneo Kitajima, Makoto Toyota, and Katsuko T. Nakahira

Beyond the Walls: Comparison of Three Extended Reality Technologies Giving Care Home Residents Access to Tourism and Cultural Content for Health and Wellbeing 63
Hannah Bradwell, Katherine Edwards, Leonie Cooper, Rory Baxter, Arunangsu Chatterjee, Ray Jones, and Catherine Hennessy

Enhancing School Visits to Museums through Gamified VR: A Complementary Approach to Learning and Social Engagement 70
Cleiton Ferreira, Paula Latorre, and Francisco Antonio Nieto-Escamez

AIVR 2025

Forward

The Second International Conference on Artificial Intelligence and Immersive Virtual Reality (AIVR 2025), held on April 6 – 10, 2025, initiated a series of events addressing the interaction between Artificial Intelligence and Virtual Reality.

Industry, agriculture, finance, health, society, education and almost all domains, including human-systems interactions (interfaces, requests, trust, ethics, etc.) are subject of major evolution with the infusion with AI-based mechanisms into Virtual environments.

Virtual environments are deemed to shape the future society. Extended virtual world will be seamlessly integrated with the physical world creating digital twins. The convergence of computing, communication, and networking for supporting complex applications (huge data, complex processing algorithms) will benefit from the Artificial Intelligence (AI) progress, especially on Deep learning, Machine learning, and Data Analytics.

This event attracted excellent contributions and active participation from all over the world. We were very pleased to receive top quality contributions.

We take here the opportunity to warmly thank all the members of the AIVR 2025 technical program committee, as well as the numerous reviewers. The creation of a high quality conference program would not have been possible without their involvement. We also kindly thank all the authors that dedicated much of their time and effort to contribute to AIVR 2025. We truly believe that, thanks to all these efforts, the final conference program consisted of top quality contributions.

Also, this event could not have been a reality without the support of many individuals, organizations and sponsors. We also gratefully thank the members of the AIVR 2025 organizing committee for their help in handling the logistics and for their work that made this professional meeting a success.

We hope AIVR 2025 was a successful international forum for the exchange of ideas and results between academia and industry and to promote further progress in the area of AI and VR. We also hope that Valencia provided a pleasant environment during the conference and everyone saved some time to enjoy this beautiful city.

AIVR 2025 Steering Committee

Muneo Kitajima, Nagaoka University of Technology (Emeritus), Japan
Manuel Caro, Universidad de Cordoba, Colombia
Carolina Cruz-Neira, University of Central Florida, USA
Aurelie Mailloux, Reims Hospital and University of Reims, France
Jerome Dinet, University of Lorraine, France
Zahra Moussavi, University of Manitoba, Canada

AIVR 2025

Committee

AIVR 2025 Steering Committee

Muneo Kitajima, Nagaoka University of Technology (Emeritus), Japan
Manuel Caro, Universidad de Cordoba, Colombia
Carolina Cruz-Neira, University of Central Florida, USA
Aurelie Mailloux, Reims Hospital and University of Reims, France
Jerome Dinet, University of Lorraine, France
Zahra Moussavi, University of Manitoba, Canada

AIVR 2025 Technical Program Committee

Suayb S. Arslan, Boğaziçi University, Turkey
Mahajan Sagar Bhaskar, Prince Sultan University (PSU), Saudi Arabia
Concettina Buccella, University of L'Aquila, Italy
Manuel Caro, Universidad de Cordoba, Colombia
Pasquale Cascarano, University of Bologna, Italy
Jean-Rémy Chardonnet, Institut Arts et Métiers de Chalon-sur-Saône | French-German Institute for Industry of the Future (ENSAM/KIT), France
Courtney D. Cogburn, Columbia University, USA
Carolina Cruz-Neira, University of Central Florida, USA
A. Augusto de Sousa, Universidade do Porto, Portugal
Jerome Dinet, University of Lorraine, France
Sai Anvesh Durvasula, Parabole.ai, USA
Christos Gatzidis, Bournemouth University, UK
Paulo Gil, NOVA School of Science and Technology, Lisbon, Portugal
Yan Hu, Blekinge Institute of Technology (BTH), Sweden
Florentine Hüttl, University Medical Center of the Johannes Gutenberg-University Mainz, Germany
Magdalena Igras-Cybulska, Interactive crafts sp. z o.o., Poland
Yirui Jiang, Cranfield University, UK
Muneo Kitajima, Nagaoka University of Technology, Japan
Nadia Magnenat-Thalmann, University of Geneva/MIRALab, Switzerland
Aurelie Mailloux, University of Reims (URCA) / Reims Hospital / 2LPN, France
Vicky McArthur, Carleton University, Canada
Sonu Mehta, Microsoft Research, India
Zahra Moussavi, University of Manitoba, Canada
Wolfgang Mueller, University of Education Weingarten, Germany
Moloud Nasiri, Converse University, USA
Michael Nkereuwem, Federal University Dutse, Nigeria
Stefania Palmieri, Politecnico di Milano, Italy
Stamatis Papadakis, University of Crete, Greece

George Papagiannakis, University of Crete, Greece
Vatesh Pasrija, Meta - Seattle, USA
Krzysztof Pietroszek, American University, Washington, USA
Ladislav Polák, Brno University of Technology, Czech Republic
Simant Prakoonwit, Bournemouth University, UK
Yiming Qiu, University of Michigan, USA
Lorenzo Stacchio, University of Bologna, Italy
Frank Steinicke, University of Hamburg, Germany
Ibrahim A. Tahmid, Virginia Tech, USA
Davide Tebaldi, University of Modena and Reggio Emilia, Italy
Yanbo Wang, Aalborg University, Denmark
Zixuan Wang, UC San Diego, USA

Copyright Information

Designing a Naturalistic and Interactive VR Museum Environment With a Realistic Avatar as a Guide for Cognitive Treatment of the Elderly

Amir Bani Saeed
Department of Biomedical Engineering
University of Manitoba
Winnipeg, Canada
banisaea@myumanitoba.ca

Zahra Moussavi
Department of Biomedical Engineering
University of Manitoba
Winnipeg, Canada
Zahra.Moussavi@umanitoba.ca

Abstract—**This project introduces a virtual reality (VR) museum designed to help individuals with cognitive impairments and memory-related challenges. A realistic avatar, created using Character Creator and animated with iClone's AccuLip tool, acts as a guide to engage users in interactive museum tours and memory exercises. The environment, which is modeled in Blender and integrated into Unity, offers an immersive experience. Users navigate the environment with the Oculus Rift, receive explanations about exhibits, and participate in recall challenges that strengthen cognitive function. A performance tracking system records user interactions, response accuracy, and time spent on tasks, providing insights into cognitive progress. By combining VR with interactive storytelling, this approach aims to improve cognitive function and reduce loneliness in the elderly. Future clinical trials will assess its effectiveness as a therapeutic tool.**

Keywords— Virtual Reality; Avatar; Cognitive impairment; Museum; loneliness.

I. INTRODUCTION

The utilization of avatars in virtual reality (VR) has emerged as a tool for addressing mental disorders, offering a unique opportunity to enhance therapeutic interventions. Previous research indicated that the usage of avatars contributed to mood change [1], self-compassion [2], and reduction in the severity of depression [3]. Despite the above advances, we still need a new generation of VR-based therapeutic methods that are automated and realistic. Recent advances in deep learning and computer vision have enabled VR systems to interactively react to humans, enhancing their realism and engagement. In this project, we focus on the development of a realistic avatar in a virtual museum to represent an individual as a guide and interact with patients. The ultimate application of this study is to utilize the naturalistic avatar of a person and a virtual museum for cognitive treatments of individuals with memory and cognitive impairments as well as depression due to loneliness.

Figure 1. An avatar based on an individual's picture in the VR museum.

II. METHOD

The avatar creation process starts with capturing a high-quality headshot, which is transformed into a realistic 3D face using Character Creator software [4]. Rigging techniques are applied to facilitate natural movements, and facial expressions are synchronized with audio using iClone's AccuLip tool [5]. These animations are then integrated into Unity using Animation State Machines, avatar masks, and root motion, ensuring smooth transitions between gestures and expressions while maintaining lifelike behavior. This allows the avatar to guide users seamlessly through the museum, offering engaging and interactive experience.

The 3D museum environment is crafted using high-resolution reference images, which are imported into Blender for modeling, texturing, and lighting. The final product is a realistic museum with detailed exhibits and artifacts, ready for user interaction.

The game development process focuses on creating scenarios that engage users in exploring various exhibits, enhancing memory recall and cognitive skills. For example, in one scenario, the user enters a room filled with paintings, and the avatar provides detailed explanations of each piece, including information about the artist, era, and significance. Afterward, the user is guided to a room with sculptures, where the avatar offers similar insights. Once both rooms are explored, the avatar challenges the user to recall specific details, such as identifying which room a particular painting was in or answering questions about the painting itself. Throughout each scenario, the avatar offers step-by-step instructions and hints to ensure that users remain engaged and can effectively engage with the content.

The Oculus Rift is used to deliver immersive VR experience, allowing users to fully engage with the environment and exhibits. This VR integration enhances the effectiveness of cognitive training, enabling users to interact naturally with the exhibits and the avatar, therefore improving engagement and memory recall. To navigate in the virtual environment, users will utilize the Oculus Rift controllers, which provide intuitive control and interaction, ensuring a seamless and interactive experience.

The user's performance is carefully tracked and recorded at each step of the process, with checkpoints to log movements, time spent at each exhibit, and interactions. Detailed logs also capture the user's responses to avatar questions, accuracy in recalling information, the time taken to complete tasks, and how often hints are requested. This data helps assessing cognitive function and engagement. A scoring system will be implemented, with points awarded based on factors such as accuracy, successful task completion, time efficiency, recall ability without hints, and overall engagement with the exhibits. Penalties will be applied for errors, excessive time, or over-reliance on hints. A cumulative score reflects the user's overall performance, providing a measure of cognitive progress.

III. CONCLUSIONS

This project is currently under development, with ongoing work in both museum environment design and game development to ensure an engaging and interactive experience. It serves as the building block for a larger program aimed at utilizing VR to enhance cognitive impairment among the elderly. The next phase, which is itself a major project, will involve testing the game on people with cognitive impairments and analyzing the data in the future. This design is expected to be used in clinical trials to explore its potential for addressing cognitive impairments as well as depression due to isolation in the aging population.

ACKNOWLEDGMENT

This work has been funded by MITAC.

REFERENCES

[1] S. Osimo, R. Pizarro, B. Spanlang, and M. Slater. Conversations between self and self as Sigmund Freud—A virtual body ownership paradigm for self counselling. Sci Rep 5, 13899 (2015). https://doi.org/10.1038/srep13899.

[2] CJ. Falconer et al. "Embodying Compassion: A Virtual Reality Paradigm for Overcoming Excessive Self-Criticism." PloS One, vol. 9, no. 11, 2014, pp. e111933–e111933, https://doi.org/10.1371/journal.pone.0111933.

[3] CJ. Falconer et al. "Embodying Self-Compassion within Virtual Reality and Its Effects on Patients with Depression." BJPsych Open, vol. 2, no. 1, 2016, pp. 74–80, https://doi.org/10.1192/bjpo.bp.115.002147.

[4] "Character Creator: 3D Character Design Software," 3D Character Maker | Character Creator | Reallusion. https://www.reallusion.com/character-creator [Accessed: 10-February-2025].

[5] "3D Animation Software | iClone | Reallusion," 3D Animation Software - iClone. https://www.reallusion.com/iclone/ [Accessed: 10-February-2025].

Non-Immersive Virtual Reality as a Safer Alternative for Cognitive Training in Older Adults: Investigating the Effect of Age on Cybersickness

Rashmita Chatterjee
Biomedical Engineering, University of Manitoba
UofM
Winnipeg, Canada
e-mail: chatter2@myumanitoba.ca

Zahra Moussavi
Biomedical Engineering, University of Manitoba
UofM
Winnipeg, Canada
e-mail: Zahra.Moussavi@umanitoba.ca

Abstract— **Virtual reality (VR) has emerged as a promising tool for cognitive training in older adults, yet cybersickness remains a significant barrier to its widespread adoption. This study investigates the effects of age and sex on cybersickness in immersive and non-immersive VR environments using data from 629 participants collected over 14 years. Participants played spatial navigation games in either an immersive (head-mounted display) or non-immersive (laptop screen) setting, and cybersickness occurrence was recorded. Logistic regression analysis revealed that in immersive VR, older age was associated with an increased likelihood of experiencing cybersickness, and females were significantly more susceptible than males. In contrast, neither age nor sex significantly influenced cybersickness occurrence in non-immersive VR, where overall cybersickness prevalence was substantially lower (6.9% vs. 24.0% in immersive VR). These findings highlight the potential of non-immersive VR as a safer and more accessible alternative for cognitive training in aging populations, mitigating the challenges posed by cybersickness in immersive VR environments.**

Keywords- virtual reality; cybersickness; age.

I. INTRODUCTION

Virtual reality (VR) has gained increasing attention as a tool for cognitive training in older adults due to its ability to provide engaging, interactive experiences that may enhance cognitive function [1–3]. However, cybersickness—a condition that presents with symptoms such as nausea, dizziness, eye fatigue, and disorientation [4]—remains a significant barrier to the widespread adoption of VR-based interventions. Cybersickness arises due to sensory mismatches between visual, vestibular, and proprioceptive inputs [5], leading to discomfort that can limit user engagement and reduce the feasibility of VR applications, particularly among older individuals.

Age has been found to influence cybersickness susceptibility [6], particularly in immersive VR environments, where users experience a greater sense of presence and motion perception. However, the directionality of the age effect remains controversial. Some studies suggest that older adults experience significantly less cybersickness than younger adults [7–9], while others report the opposite, with older individuals being more vulnerable [10, 11]. Most existing studies have been limited by small sample sizes, making it difficult to draw definitive conclusions. Additionally, while the impact of age on cybersickness has been explored in immersive VR environments, there is a lack of research on non-immersive VR systems, such as those using conventional screens (e.g., laptops or desktop monitors), which are widely available and often more accessible for older adults. Understanding how cybersickness manifests in non-immersive VR settings is critical, especially since these systems could serve as a safer and more practical alternative for cognitive training in aging populations. To address this gap, we conducted a large-scale analysis using data collected over 14 years from 629 participants, evaluating the effect of age and sex on cybersickness in both immersive and non-immersive VR environments.

II. METHOD

Participants played one of three VR-based spatial navigation games: VRNHouse, Virtual Hallway, or Barn Ruins. These games involved maze-like route-finding tasks designed for spatial navigation studies and had been tested and validated in previous research. Participants played either immersive games using a head-mounted display (HMD) or non-immersive games on a laptop screen using a gaming controller. Their age, sex, and cybersickness occurrence (binary: present/absent) were recorded. As shown in Table I, the immersive VR group consisted of 179 participants (mean age: 55.84 ± 19.65 years, 70 males), while the non-immersive VR group included 450 participants (mean age: 56.56 ± 17.85 years, 159 males). Given that cybersickness is influenced by the level of immersion, we conducted separate logistic regression analyses for the immersive and non-immersive datasets to examine the effects of age and sex on the likelihood of experiencing cybersickness. Logistic regression was used as the outcome measure- cybersickness occurrence- was binary.

III. RESULTS

The logistic regression analysis for the immersive group (n = 179) showed that both age and sex significantly influenced cybersickness occurrence. Among the 179 participants, 43 (24.0%) reported experiencing cybersickness, while 136 (76.0%) did not, as outlined in Table I. Sex had a significant effect (OR = 0.17, 95% CI [0.06, 0.41], $p < 0.001$), indicating that males were significantly less likely to experience cybersickness than females. Additionally, for every 10-year increase in age, the odds of experiencing cybersickness increased by 1.28 times (OR = 1.28, 95% CI [1.04, 1.61], p = 0.024).

Conversely, in the non-immersive VR group (n = 450), only 31 participants (6.9%) reported cybersickness, while 419 (93.1%) did not. Logistic regression revealed that neither age nor sex had a significant effect on cybersickness susceptibility in non-immersive VR.

TABLE I. DESCRIPTIVE STATISTICS FOR FACTORS IMPACTING CYBERSICKNESS SUSCEPTIBILITY IN VERBAL IMMERSIVE AND NON-IMMERSIVE DATA (MEANS ± SD)

	Verbal-immersive full dataset	*Verbal-nonimmersive subset*
N	179	450
CS (present/ absent)	43/136	31/419
Age	55.84 ± 19.65	56.56 ± 17.85
Sex (Male/Female)	70/109	159/291

IV. CONCLUSION

Our findings suggest that older adults face a higher risk of cybersickness in immersive VR environments, congruent with the results in the studies [10, 11]. This increased risk could limit their ability to comfortably engage with immersive VR-based cognitive training programs. Our study did not find this increased risk of cybersickness in older adults while using non-immersive VR, making it a safer and more viable alternative for prolonged cognitive training sessions.

These findings have important implications for the design of VR-based cognitive training programs for older adults. While immersive VR is engaging and realistic, older adults are more likely to experience cybersickness while using immersive technology. This may make it harder for them to use VR headsets for long periods, reducing their ability to stick with VR-based cognitive training programs. In contrast, non-immersive VR had a significantly lower incidence of cybersickness (6.9%), reinforcing its potential as a more comfortable and accessible alternative for older users.

By prioritizing non-immersive VR solutions, cognitive training programs can maximize engagement and accessibility while minimizing the discomfort associated with cybersickness, ultimately improving the overall effectiveness of VR-based cognitive rehabilitation for older adults.

V. STUDY LIMITATIONS AND FUTURE WORK

This study is limited by the specific VR games used, the lack of a control group, and the exclusion of factors such as prior VR experience, motion sickness susceptibility, and personality traits. Future research should investigate a wider range of VR applications, examine individual differences in cybersickness susceptibility, and explore adaptive strategies to reduce discomfort in immersive VR. Additionally, long-term studies are needed to evaluate the effectiveness, engagement, and feasibility of non-immersive VR for cognitive training in older adults, particularly in real-world and clinical settings.

ACKNOWLEDGMENT

The studies from which the cybersickness data used in this paper were derived were all supported by NSERC.

REFERENCES

[1] R. I. García-Betances, V. Jiménez-Mixco, M. T. Arredondo, and M. F. Cabrera-Umpiérrez, "Using virtual reality for cognitive training of the elderly," Am J Alzheimers Dis Other Demen, vol. 30, no. 1, pp. 49–54, 2015, doi: 10.1177/1533317514545866.

[2] Y. Zhou et al., "The Current Research of Spatial Cognitive Evaluation and Training With Brain–Computer Interface and Virtual Reality," Front Neurosci, vol. 13, no. February, pp. 1–5, 2020, doi: 10.3389/fnins.2019.01439.

[3] K. Harrington, M. P. Craven, M. L. Wilson, and A. Landowska, "Perceptions of Cognitive Training Games and Assessment Technologies for Dementia: Acceptability Study With Patient and Public Involvement Workshops," JMIR Serious Games, vol. 10, no. 2, Jun. 2022, doi: 10.2196/32489.

[4] R. S. Kennedy, N. E. Lane, K. S. Berbaum, and M. G. Lilienthal, "Simulator Sickness Questionnaire: An Enhanced Method for Quantifying Simulator Sickness," Int J Aviat Psychol, vol. 3, no. 3, pp. 203–220, 1993, doi: 10.1207/S15327108IJAP0303_3.

[5] J. T. Reason, "Motion sickness adaptation: A neural mismatch model," J R Soc Med, vol. 71, no. 11, 1978, doi: 10.1177/014107687807101109.

[6] N. Biswas, A. Mukherjee, and S. Bhattacharya, "'Are you feeling sick?' – A systematic literature review of cybersickness in virtual reality," ACM Comput Surv, vol. 56, no. 11, pp. 1–38, Nov. 2024, doi: 10.1145/3670008.

[7] A. T. Dilanchian, R. Andringa, and W. R. Boot, "A Pilot Study Exploring Age Differences in Presence, Workload, and Cybersickness in the Experience of Immersive Virtual Reality Environments," Front Virtual Real, vol. 2, Oct. 2021, doi: 10.3389/frvir.2021.736793.

[8] D. Saredakis, A. Szpak, B. Birckhead, H. A. D Keage, A. Rizzo, and T. Loetscher, "Factors Associated With Virtual Reality Sickness in Head-Mounted Displays: A Systematic Review and Meta-Analysis," Frontiers in Human Neuroscience | www.frontiersin.org, vol. 14, p. 96, 2020, doi: 10.3389/fnhum.2020.00096.

[9] L. E. Garrido et al., "Focusing on cybersickness: pervasiveness, latent trajectories, susceptibility, and effects on the virtual reality experience," Virtual Real, vol. 26, no. 4, pp. 1347–1371, Dec. 2022, doi: 10.1007/s10055-022-00636-4.

[10] B. Keshavarz, R. Ramkhalawansingh, B. Haycock, S. Shahab, and J. L. Campos, "Comparing simulator sickness in younger and older adults during simulated driving under different multisensory conditions," Transp Res Part F Traffic Psychol Behav, vol. 54, pp. 47–62, Apr. 2018, doi: 10.1016/J.TRF.2018.01.007.

[11] H. Oh and W. Son, "Cybersickness and Its Severity Arising from Virtual Reality Content: A Comprehensive Study," Sensors, vol. 22, no. 4, Feb. 2022, doi: 10.3390/s22041314.

Acceptability of an AI-Powered Wearable Ring Sensor for Upper Body Mobility in Individuals with Cognitive Impairment: A Pilot Study

Holly Shannon[a], Asma Seraj Pour Shooshtari[b], Logan Young[c], Makara Rolle[c], Jennifer O'Neil[d,e], Jose Carlos Tatmatsu-Rocha[f], Dahlia Kairy[g,h], Olga Theou[j], Zahra Moussavi[b,k], Ke Peng[b,k], Mirella Veras[c,h,i,k,l]*

[a]Department of Neuroscience, Carleton University, Ottawa, Ontario, Canada
[b]Department of Electrical and Computer Engineering, Price Faculty of Engineering, University of Manitoba, Winnipeg, Manitoba, Canada
[c]Department of Health Science, Carleton University, Ottawa, Ontario, Canada
[d]School of Rehabilitation Sciences, Faculty of Health Sciences, University of Ottawa, Ottawa, Ontario, Canada
[e]Bruyère Health Research Institute, Ottawa, Ontario, Canada
[f]College of Medicine, Federal University of Ceará-UFC, Ceará, Brazil
[g]École de Réadaptation, Faculté de Médecine, Université de Montréal, Montréal, Québec, Canada
[h]Centre for Interdisciplinary Research in Rehabilitation of Greater Montreal, Montréal, Québec, Canada
[i]Department of Physical Therapy, College of Rehabilitation Sciences, Rady Faculty of Health Sciences, University of Manitoba, Winnipeg, Manitoba, Canada
[j]School of Physiotherapy, Dalhousie University, Halifax, Nova Scotia, Canada
[k]Riverview Health Centre, Winnipeg, Manitoba, Canada
[l]Centre on Aging, University of Manitoba, Winnipeg, Manitoba, Canada
e-mail: hollyshannon@cmail.carleton.ca, serajpoa@myumanitoba.ca, loganyoung@cmail.carleton.ca, makararolle@cmail.carleton.ca, joneil@uottawa.ca, tatmatsu@ufc.br, dahlia.kairy@umontreal.ca, olga.theou@dal.ca, zahra.moussavi@umanitoba.ca, ke.peng@umanitoba.ca, mirella.veras@umanitoba.ca
*Corresponding author: mirella.veras@umanitoba.ca

***Abstract*—Dementia affects cognitive function and daily functioning, with an increasing global prevalence. This pilot study assesses the feasibility, usability, and acceptance of a wearable ring powered by Artificial Intelligence (AI) to monitor upper body movements in individuals with dementia. After wearing the device for one full day, all participants adhered to the device. Quantitative results revealed moderate usability and acceptance. Qualitative themes included high comfort, low perceived significance, and minimal impact on daily activities. This study demonstrates the feasibility of an AI-powered wearable device in dementia care. Future large-scale studies should incorporate individuals with different levels of cognitive disability to assess the adaptability of wearable technology to their needs.**

Keywords--Wearable Devices; Artificial Intelligence; Dementia; Feasibility; Aging; Movement Monitoring.

I. Introduction

Dementia impacts memory, cognition, behavior, and daily tasks, affecting 36.5 million people globally [1][2]. People with dementia and cognitive disabilities have historically been excluded from research, especially in gerontology, reflecting broader ableism that marginalizes those with dementia [3]. Over the past decade, there has been a growing shift toward addressing these biases, emphasizing the importance of inclusive health technology research to ensure equitable access, use, and benefits from technological advancements [4][5]. This shift is crucial in advancing technologies like wearable devices, which can enhance dementia care [6]. Kinematic technologies—such as accelerometers, Global Positioning System (GPS) trackers, and motion detection tools—offer cost-effective, minimally invasive ways to assess disease burden and deliver personalized care [6]. Wearable devices provide continuous physiological monitoring in real-world settings, offering insights beyond traditional in-clinic assessments. These technologies support rehabilitation, measure mobility, and improve daily functioning in aging populations [7]. However, the current use of wearable devices in dementia patients is primarily utilized for measurement of the sleep wake cycle [5]. Artificial intelligence (AI) enhances dementia management through AI-powered wearables and telepresence systems, providing cognitive support, and social engagement [8]. These innovations reduce the caregiver burden, improve patient well-being, and enable real-time, personalized health monitoring [8][9]. Expanding on these advancements, AI-integrated wearable devices, such as a ring sensor for shoulder movement monitoring, present a promising tool for supporting individuals with dementia [9]. This study aims to assess the feasibility, usability, and acceptance of a wearable ring powered with AI designed to track upper body movements in individuals with dementia. The rest of the paper is structured as follows. In Section II, we present the methods pertaining to quantitative and qualitative data collection. In Section III, we outline feasibility, acceptability and usability results of the pilot study. Finally, Section IV addresses the conclusions and future work directions.

II. METHODS

This pilot study employed a mixed methods design to assess the feasibility, acceptability, and usability of wearable sensor technology for older adults with dementia. Quantitative methods were used to evaluate feasibility and usability, followed by a qualitative phase using a focus group to explore participant experiences. Participants were recruited from a long-term care home using convenience sampling. Eligibility criteria required participants to be aged 65 or older, residing in the facility, and capable of providing informed consent. Exclusion criteria included significant mobility restrictions or medical conditions affecting sensor use, such as severe arthritis, hand tremors, or Raynaud's disease. The intervention involved participants wearing a ring-based wearable sensor to continuously monitor upper-body movements. Participants wore the device for one day, from 8:30 AM to 3:30 PM (Figure 1). A trained staff member ensured proper device usage and data integrity. The XO TECHNOLOGY© ring, linked to the XO HEALTH© app on Android and iOS tablets, collected and analyzed movement data using AI algorithms [10].

Figure 1. Wearable ring devices by XO technology.

Metrics included shoulder flexion, extension, abduction, adduction, and rotational movements. The AI-driven platform identified anomalies and provided insights to support early detection of movement limitations. Quantitative data collection assessed feasibility through adherence tracking and usability via the Technology Acceptance Questionnaire (TAQ) and User Acceptance Questionnaire (UAQ) [11][12]. One week post-intervention, a structured focus group was conducted to explore participant perceptions of comfort, ease of use, and impact on daily activities.

III. RESULTS

The final sample included five participants with moderate dementia (Table 1). Cognitive status scores on the Mini-Mental State Examination ranged from 5 to 30, with a mean score of 20.90 (SD ±8.84). The feasibility of the device was demonstrated, as all residents used it correctly, and no residents requested to remove the ring. However, an issue arose when the ring sensor size was too large for one participant. Questionnaire results indicate moderate usability and acceptance, with mean scores of 52.20 (SD ±38.40) on the TAQ and 87.80 (SD ±66.20) on the UAQ. Qualitative analysis identified three key themes: High Ring Comfortability, with participants finding the ring comfortable due to its design; Low Ring Significance, as many felt the ring had little noticeable impact or benefit; and Low Ring Impact, as it did not interfere with daily activities like exercising or showering. The wearable ring is designed to monitor upper body movement in individuals with dementia, providing data on their physical activity, mobility patterns, and potential early frailty indicators.

TABLE 1: CHARACTERISTICS OF STUDY PARTICIPANTS

Category	Dementia (n=5)
Gender	
Female	4 (80.0%)
Male	1 (20.0%)
Duration (in seconds)	1703.00 ± 348.00
Ethnicity	
White	5 (100.0%)
Other	0 (0.0%)
Highest Level of Education	
High School or Equivalent	4 (80.0%)
Other	1 (20.0%)
Engaged in Recreational Activities Involving Shoulder Exercises Today?	
No	0 (0.0%)
Yes	5 (100.0%)
Expressed Shoulder Pain Today?	
No	4 (80.0%)
Yes	1 (20.0%)
Expressed Discomfort with the Device?	
No	4 (80.0%)
Yes	1 (20.0%)
Age (Mean ± SD)	78.60 ± 81.60

Movement monitoring can help assess motor function, detect changes that may signal increased fall risk, and support personalized interventions. Establishing the acceptability of this technology is a crucial step toward its integration into dementia care, ensuring its feasibility for real-world application. This study is not without limitation. Exclusionary criteria were made to ensure accuracy and reliability of data collection; however, this may not fully represent the experience of individuals with more advanced physical impairments. This limits the generalizability of the results to a broader population of people with dementia.

IV. CONCLUSION AND FUTURE WORK

This study shows the feasibility and potential of AI-powered wearable ring technology for individuals with dementia. Participants wore the device consistently, with minimal discomfort, demonstrating its acceptability and practicality. The design features prioritize ease of use, adaptability, and low intrusiveness, which enhanced its usability. Future large-scale studies should include individuals with varying levels of cognitive disability to evaluate how wearable technology can be adapted to meet their needs. This would expand the generalizability of findings and better address the diverse experiences of people living with dementia. Finally, future research should explore the use of the ring device in other conditions outside of dementia to further examine generalizability of the ring device.

REFERENCES

[1] World Health Organization. "Dementia." https://www.who.int/news-room/fact-sheets/detail/dementia.

[2] G. Livingston *et al.*, "Dementia prevention, intervention, and care: 2024 report of the Lancet standing Commission," (in eng), *Lancet*, vol. 404, no. 10452, pp. 572-628, Aug 10 2024, doi: 10.1016/s0140-6736(24)01296-0.

[3] J. Taylor, S. Demers, E. Vig, and S. Borson, "The Disappearing Subject: Exclusion of People with Cognitive Impairment and Dementia from Geriatrics Research," *Journal of the American Geriatrics Society*, vol. 60, pp. 413-9, 01/30 2012, doi: 10.1111/j.1532-5415.2011.03847.x.

[4] J. S. Yi, C. A. Pittman, C. L. Price, C. L. Nieman, and E. S. Oh, "Telemedicine and Dementia Care: A Systematic Review of Barriers and Facilitators," (in eng), *J Am Med Dir Assoc*, vol. 22, no. 7, pp. 1396-1402.e18, Jul 2021, doi: 10.1016/j.jamda.2021.03.015.

[5] A. C. Cote, R. J. Phelps, N. S. Kabiri, J. S. Bhangu, and K. K. Thomas, "Evaluation of Wearable Technology in Dementia: A Systematic Review and Meta-Analysis," (in eng), *Front Med (Lausanne)*, vol. 7, p. 501104, 2020, doi: 10.3389/fmed.2020.501104.

[6] I. C. Rocha *et al.*, "Monitoring Wearable Devices for Elderly People with Dementia: A Review," *Designs*, vol. 8, no. 4, doi: 10.3390/designs8040075.

[7] A. Carnevale *et al.*, "Wearable systems for shoulder kinematics assessment: a systematic review," (in eng), *BMC Musculoskelet Disord*, vol. 20, no. 1, p. 546, Nov 15 2019, doi: 10.1186/s12891-019-2930-4.

[8] J. Qi, C. Wu, L. Yang, C. Ni, and Y. Liu, "Artificial intelligence (AI) for home support interventions in dementia: a scoping review protocol," (in eng), *BMJ Open*, vol. 12, no. 9, p. e062604, Sep 21 2022, doi: 10.1136/bmjopen-2022-062604.

[9] S. Shajari, K. Kuruvinashetti, A. Komeili, and U. Sundararaj, "The Emergence of AI-Based Wearable Sensors for Digital Health Technology: A Review," (in eng), *Sensors (Basel)*, vol. 23, no. 23, Nov 29 2023

[10] XO Ring. https://www.xotechnology.ca/

[11] F. D. Davis, "Perceived Usefulness, Perceived Ease of Use, and User Acceptance of Information Technology." *MIS Quarterly*, vol. 13, no. 3, 1989, pp. 319–40. *JSTOR*, https://doi.org/10.2307/249008.

[12] A. Spagnolli, E. Guardigli, V. Orso, A. Varotto, L. Gamberini, " Measuring User Acceptance of Wearable Symbiotic Devices: Validation Study Across Application Scenarios." In: Jacucci, G., Gamberini, L., Freeman, J., Spagnolli, A. (eds) Symbiotic Interaction. Symbiotic 2015. Lecture Notes in Computer Science(), vol 8820. Springer, Cham. https://doi.org/10.1007/978-3-319-13500-

Extended Reality (XR) vs. Virtual Reality (VR) for Artificial Intelligence (AI)-Driven Balance Improvement in Older Adults

Mirella Veras[a]*, Asma Seraj Pour Shooshtari[b], Zahra Moussavi[b,c], and Ke Peng[b,c]
[a]Department of Physical Therapy, College of Rehabilitation Sciences,
University of Manitoba, Winnipeg, Manitoba, Canada
[b]Department of Electrical and Computer Engineering, Price Faculty of Engineering,
University of Manitoba, Winnipeg, Manitoba, Canada
[c]Riverview Health Centre, Winnipeg, Manitoba, Canada
e-mail: mirella.veras@umanitoba.ca, serajpoa@myumanitoba.ca,
zahra.moussavi@umanitoba.ca, ke.peng@umanitoba.ca
*Corresponding author: mirella.veras@umanitoba.ca

Abstract—**Balance impairment in older adults significantly increases fall risk, leading to decreased mobility, higher healthcare expenditures, and reduced quality of life. The emergence of rehabilitation technologies such as Virtual Reality (VR) and Extended Reality (XR), enhanced with Artificial Intelligence (AI), offers promising interventions to mitigate these risks. VR provides immersive, controlled environments suitable for structured rehabilitation programs, whereas XR integrates real-world scenarios, facilitating functional mobility training applicable in home and community settings. Despite their potential, evidence comparing the effectiveness, adaptability, and clinical applicability of AI-enhanced VR and XR interventions for balance rehabilitation remains limited. This rapid systematic review protocol outlines a structured approach to evaluating existing literature through comprehensive database searches, clearly defined inclusion criteria, and systematic narrative synthesis informed by the Metaverse Equitable Rehabilitation Therapy (MERTH) framework. The findings of this research will not only clarify the comparative advantages, barriers, and limitations of VR and XR technologies but also identify evidence-based best practices and propose recommendations to guide future clinical practice and technology development in balance rehabilitation for older adults. This research is crucial in shaping the future of rehabilitation for older adults and is of significant interest to the healthcare community.**

Keywords- Balance; Artificial Intelligence; Virtual Reality; Extended Reality; Aging; Fall Prevention; Older Adults; Review.

I. INTRODUCTION

Balance impairments among older adults present significant risks, including increased incidence of falls, reduced mobility, and a greater probability of hospitalization due to injuries [1]. As the global population ages, the potential of innovative technologies to enhance balance rehabilitation and mitigate fall risks among older adults is becoming increasingly clear [1]. Virtual Reality (VR) and Extended Reality (XR) are effective technologies that provide immersive, interactive, and engaging environments for tailored balance rehabilitation programs [2][3][4]. VR utilizes fully immersive, computer-generated environments to isolate users from real-world distractions, enabling structured and precisely controlled rehabilitation experiences. In contrast, XR technology combines real-world settings with virtual augmentations, providing a hybrid environment that supports functional and context-driven rehabilitation exercises relevant to daily activities [2]. The integration of Artificial Intelligence (AI) further enhances these technologies, enabling personalized exercise programs, real-time movement analysis, adaptive feedback, and dynamic adjustment of exercises tailored to individual performance and needs [5]. Despite their potential, VR and XR's comparative effectiveness, adaptability, and clinical applicability within AI-enhanced balance rehabilitation interventions have not been sufficiently studied. This abstract summarizes a proposal to conduct a rapid, systematic review of recent literature to evaluate and compare the effectiveness, adaptability, and clinical utility of VR and XR technologies integrated with AI for balance rehabilitation among older adults. The goal is to identify the optimal technology for improving balance and reducing fall risk across different environments. The structure of the paper is as follows: Section II details the methodology used to perform this rapid review, including search strategy, inclusion and exclusion criteria, data extraction processes, and quality assessment considerations. Section III outlines the planned synthesis and presentation of results, including the comparison criteria of effectiveness, adaptability, and clinical applicability. Section IV discusses how the findings from this review can inform the design and implementation of future AI-enhanced VR and XR rehabilitation programs. Finally, Section V presents the conclusion, summarizing key understandings, identifying existing gaps in the current literature, and proposing future research to improve technology-enhanced balance rehabilitation interventions for older adults.

II. METHODS

This rapid systematic review will utilize the Population, Intervention, Comparison, and Outcomes (PICO) framework [6] to define the study's scope, clearly identifying the population, intervention, comparison, and outcomes of interest. Specifically, the population includes older adults ($\geq$ 65 years) experiencing balance impairment or increased fall risk. Compared with traditional or non-AI-assisted rehabilitation methods, the interventions under consideration are AI-enhanced Virtual Reality (VR) and Extended Reality (XR) rehabilitation technologies. The outcomes assessed include balance improvement, fall risk reduction, personalized adaptation, patient engagement and compliance, clinical feasibility, cost-effectiveness, and sustained functional gains.

To guide a comprehensive analysis, the review will apply the Metaverse Equitable Rehabilitation Therapy (MERTH) framework [7], which consists of five domains: Equity, Health Services Integration, Technological Adaptation, Global Governance, and Humanization, each domain is further divided into relevant subdomains (Figure 1). The MERTH framework will ensure that the systematic review addresses critical issues of accessibility, inclusivity, diversity, fairness, cultural relevance, adaptability, clinical feasibility, patient engagement, and the broader ethical considerations of implementing VR and XR rehabilitation interventions in clinical practice.

A systematic literature search will be conducted in several databases, such as PubMed, Scopus, and IEEE Xplore, focusing on peer-reviewed studies published within the past five years. The search will specifically target studies evaluating AI-driven VR or XR balance rehabilitation interventions compared to traditional rehabilitation programs or those without AI enhancements. Data extraction will focus on intervention characteristics (exercise programs, real-time movement analysis, adaptive feedback, and dynamic adjustments tailored to individual performance and needs), study design, patient demographics, and outcomes (Table I).

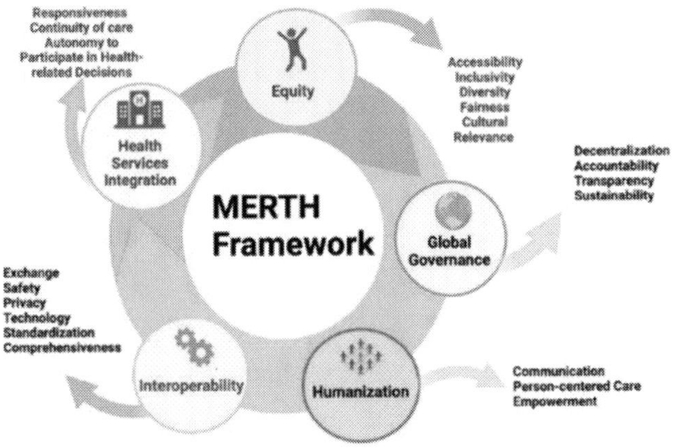

Figure 1: Metaverse Equitable Rehabilitation Therapy (MERTH) framework.

A. *Screening and Data Extraction*

Two independent reviewers will conduct study screening, full-text review, data extraction, and quality assessment, guided by the predefined categories of the MERTH framework and the PICO structure. In discrepancies, consensus will be sought through reviewer discussion, with the involvement of a third reviewer when necessary. Data extracted will include key study characteristics such as AI tools used, intervention type (VR or XR), study population, research design, measured outcomes, and primary results. A standardized extraction template will document additional data on study settings, sample characteristics, and methodological rigor. Equity, ethics, safety, confidentiality, and privacy considerations associated with AI-driven rehabilitation interventions will also be evaluated systematically. Extracted data will be managed and coded using the Covidence Software [8], facilitating comprehensive and accurate analysis.

TABLE I: POTENTIAL OUTCOMES IN VR AND XR AI-DRIVEN BALANCE REHABILITATION.

Outcome	Description	Measurement/Indicator
Balance Improvement	Assess the impact of VR and XR technologies on postural stability, fall prevention, and functional balance in older adults.	Berg Balance Scale (BBS), Timed Up and Go (TUG) test, Functional Reach Test (FRT), reduction in fall frequency.
Personalized Adaptation	Evaluate how effectively VR/XR technologies tailor rehabilitation exercises based on individual motor function, cognitive status, and progression.	AI-driven progression metrics, modified exercise difficulty levels, user-reported adaptability via standardized questionnaires (e.g., System Usability Scale)
Clinical Feasibility	Determine the practicality of implementing VR/XR in rehabilitation, long-term care, and home rehabilitation settings.	Healthcare provider feedback (standardized surveys), cost-effectiveness analysis, adherence rates in real-world use
User Engagement and Compliance	Measure patient engagement, motivation, and VR/XR rehabilitation protocol adherence.	Participant-reported engagement scores (e.g., Intrinsic Motivation Inventory), session completion rates, dropout rates
Cost-effectiveness	Compare the financial viability of VR/XR-based rehabilitation against traditional rehabilitation interventions.	Cost-benefit analysis, direct treatment costs, healthcare savings from fall prevention
Sustained Functional Gains	Assess long-term retention of balance and mobility improvements post-intervention.	Follow-up assessments at 6 months and 1 year using BBS, TUG, Activities-specific Balance Confidence (ABC) scale, incidence of falls

B. *Assessment of the Risk of Bias (RoB)*

Two reviewers will independently assess the Risk of Bias (RoB) of the included systematic reviews and primary studies. Discrepancies between reviewers will be resolved through discussion. For the systematic reviews, the AMSTAR-2 Checklist [9] will be applied, evaluating critical methodological domains, including eligibility criteria, comprehensiveness of literature searches, data extraction, quality of study appraisal, and clarity of findings synthesis. Each domain will be categorized as having low, unclear, or high RoB. For primary studies, randomized controlled trials (RCTs) will be assessed using the Cochrane Risk of Bias 2 (RoB 2) tool [10], and observational or non-randomized studies will be evaluated using the Risk of Bias in Non-randomized Studies of Interventions (ROBINS-I) tool [11].

III. Results

Findings from this rapid review will be narratively synthesized following the five domains of the MERTH framework, encompassing equity, integration of health services, technological adaptation, global governance, and humanization. Results will systematically evaluate AI-enhanced VR and XR rehabilitation interventions' effectiveness, adaptability, clinical applicability, and equity considerations. Subgroup analyses will explore variations according to population characteristics (e.g. age, gender, socioeconomic status), intervention types (exercise programs, assessment tools, gamification strategies), and equity dimensions (accessibility, inclusivity, cultural relevance). The review will highlight strengths, limitations, implementation barriers, and equity issues aligned with MERTH domains, ensuring a comprehensive assessment. The reporting will follow the PRISMA-AI [12] guidelines to maintain rigor, transparency, and clarity.

IV. Discussion

The methodology of this rapid systematic review presents potential challenges that can affect the feasibility, data reliability, and overall strength of the findings. One limitation is the availability and quality of existing literature, as AI-enhanced VR and XR applications for balance rehabilitation remain an emerging field with limited high-quality randomized controlled trials. Many studies may have small sample sizes, inconsistent methodologies, or lack rigorous comparative analysis between VR, XR, and traditional rehabilitation approaches. Standardizing outcome measures remains challenging since researchers use varied clinical tools, motion analysis systems, and patient-reported outcomes to assess balance improvement and fall risk reduction, complicating data synthesis across studies. Risk of bias assessment can highlight inconsistencies, particularly in non-randomized studies, where uncontrolled factors such as participant adherence, therapist involvement, or environmental settings may influence intervention effects. Relying on databases such as PubMed, Scopus, and IEEE Xplore can also introduce publication bias by underrepresenting studies with negative or neutral findings. Feasibility concerns affect AI-driven VR and XR interventions' broader clinical and real-world applicability. These technologies perform well in controlled environments, but cost, accessibility, clinician training, and patient adoption create barriers to real-world implementation. The team applies its expertise in knowledge synthesis to rigorously mitigate these challenges.

V. Conclusion and Future work

This rapid review protocol summarizes a methodology to systematically evaluate the integration of AI with Virtual Reality and Extended Reality technologies in balance rehabilitation interventions for older adults. The synthesis of current evidence will clarify these technologies' comparative effectiveness, adaptability, feasibility, and clinical applicability. Furthermore, the review will identify the strengths, limitations, and implementation barriers of VR and XR interventions, explicitly addressing equity considerations guided by the MERTH framework. The findings from this analysis will help guide future research, inform clinical practice, and support the development of equitable, accessible, and evidence-based rehabilitation interventions to reduce fall risks and enhance functional mobility among older adults.

References

[1] M. K. Appeadu and B. Bordoni, *Falls and Fall Prevention in Older Adults*. Treasure Island (FL): StatPearls Publishing, Jun. 2023, PMID: 32809596.

[2] A. Nishchyk, W. Chen, A. Pripp, and A. Bergland, "The effect of mixed reality technologies for falls prevention among older adults: Systematic review and meta-analysis," *JMIR Aging*, vol. 4, no. 2, e27972, Jun. 2021, PMID: 34255643; PMCID: PMC8280833. DOI: 10.2196/27972.

[3] M. Veras, D. Kairy, M. Rogante, C. Giacomozzi, and S. Saraiva, "Scoping review of outcome measures used in telerehabilitation and virtual reality for post-stroke rehabilitation," *Journal of Telemedicine and Telecare*, vol. 23, no. 6, pp. 567–587, 2017, PMID: 27342850. DOI: 10 . 1177 / 1357633X16656235.

[4] L. A. M. Montilla *et al.*, "Effectiveness of virtual reality in balance training for fall prevention in older adults: Systematic review," *Sports Medicine and Arthroscopy Review*, vol. 31, no. 2, 2023, PMID: 37418173. DOI: 10.1097/JSA.0000000000000367.

[5] M. Veras *et al.*, "A protocol for ai-powered tools to enhance mobility and function in older adults: An evidence and gap map," *Journal of Personalized Medicine*, vol. 15, no. 1, p. 29, 2025. DOI: 10.3390/jpm15010029.

[6] D. B. Matchar, "Chapter 1: Introduction to the methods guide for medical test reviews," *Journal of General Internal Medicine*, vol. 27, no. Suppl 1, S4–S10, Jun. 2012. DOI: 10.1007/s11606-011-1798-2.

[7] M. Veras *et al.*, "A framework for equitable virtual rehabilitation in the metaverse era: Challenges and opportunities," *Front Rehabil Sci*, vol. 4, p. 1 241 020, 2023, PMID: 37691912; PMCID: PMC10488814. DOI: 10.3389/fresc.2023.1241020.

[8] C. S. R. Software, *Covidence systematic review software*, https://www.covidence.org, Accessed on 20 February 2023, Melbourne, Australia: Veritas Health Innovation, 2023.

[9] B. J. Shea, B. C. Reeves, G. Wells, and et al., "Amstar 2 is a critical appraisal tool for systematic reviews that includes randomised or non-randomised studies of healthcare interventions, or both," *BMJ*, vol. 358, j4008, 2017. DOI: 10.1136/bmj.j4008.

[10] J. A. C. Sterne *et al.*, "Rob 2: A revised tool for assessing risk of bias in randomised trials," *BMJ*, vol. 366, p. l4898, 2019. DOI: 10.1136/bmj.l4898.

[11] J. A. Sterne *et al.*, "Robins-i: A tool for assessing risk of bias in non-randomised studies of interventions," *BMJ*, vol. 355, p. i4919, 2016. DOI: 10.1136/bmj.i4919.

[12] G. E. Cacciamani, T. N. Chu, D. I. Sanford, and et al., "Prisma-ai reporting guidelines for systematic reviews and meta-analyses on ai in healthcare," *Nature Medicine*, vol. 29, pp. 14–15, 2023. DOI: 10.1038/s41591-022-02139-w.

Employing Optical Brain Imaging for Real-Time Assessment of Brain Functions During Immersive Virtual Reality: Harnessing Potential for Neurorehabilitation

Asma Seraj Pour Shooshtari[a], Mirella Veras[b], Ali Kassab[c], Daniel Alejandro Galindo Lazo[c], Frédéric Lesage[d], Dang Khoa Nguyen[e], Zahra Moussavi[a,f], and Ke Peng[a,f]*
[a]Department of Electrical and Computer Engineering, Price Faculty of Engineering,
University of Manitoba, Winnipeg, Manitoba, Canada
[b]Department of Physical Therapy, College of Rehabilitation Sciences,
University of Manitoba, Winnipeg, Manitoba, Canada
[c]Department of Neurosciences, University of Montreal, Montreal, Quebec, Canada
[d]Institute of Biomedical Engineering, Polytechnique Montreal, Montreal, Quebec, Canada
[e]Department of Neurology, Research Center of the University of Montreal Hospital Center (CRCHUM),
Montreal, Quebec, Canada
[f]Riverview Health Centre, Winnipeg, Manitoba, Canada
e-mail: serajpoa@myumanitoba.ca, mirella.veras@umanitoba.ca, ali.kassab@umontreal.ca,
daniel.alejandro.galindo.lazo@umontreal.ca, frederic.lesage@polymtl.ca,
d.nguyen@umontreal.ca, zahra.moussavi@umanitoba.ca, ke.peng@umanitoba.ca
*Corresponding author: ke.peng@umanitoba.ca

Abstract—**This ongoing study introduces a cutting-edge integration of immersive Virtual Reality (iVR) and functional Near-Infrared Spectroscopy (fNIRS) to facilitate real-time monitoring of brain activity during iVR-based tasks. By combining a High Tech Computer Corporation (HTC) Vive Pro VR headset with a multichannel fNIRS system, the platform provides a portable, non-invasive solution for investigating motor and cognitive control functions under immersive conditions. The study focuses on tasks that mimic real-world rehabilitation exercises, such as hand-grasping movements, designed to engage both motor and executive brain regions. Preliminary results from two healthy participants demonstrate robust hemodynamic responses in the Bilateral Motor Cortices (M1) and Dorso-Lateral Pre-Frontal Cortices (DLPFC) during iVR tasks, revealing increased neural activation compared to similar tasks performed in real-world and screen-based environments. Enhanced functional connectivity between the M1 and DLPFC was also observed, suggesting improved coordination of motor and cognitive processes. These findings highlight the potential of the iVR-fNIRS platform to capture unique patterns of brain engagement and functional activation during immersive virtual tasks. This novel approach addresses a critical gap in neurorehabilitation research by enabling continuous, real-time assessment of brain activity during therapy. The platform's portability and resilience to motion make it well-suited for clinical applications, including personalized rehabilitation programs for patients with neurological conditions. Future work will extend the study to larger populations and incorporate additional cognitive tasks to validate the platform's versatility and reliability. This research paves the way for innovative neuroscience tools and therapeutic interventions driven by Artificial Intelligence (AI), enhancing our ability to monitor and optimize brain function in immersive virtual environments.**

Keywords-Immersive Virtual Reality (iVR); Functional Near-Infrared Spectroscopy (fNIRS); Neurorehabilitation; Hemodynamic Response.

I. Introduction

Immersive Virtual Reality (iVR) has been increasingly recognized as a promising tool in neuroscience research and therapeutic interventions for neurological disorders [1]. By integrating various visual, auditory, and haptic stimuli, iVR creates an engaging and interactive virtual environment that simulates real-world interactions. This offers an unprecedented opportunity for cognitive and physical function training for many neurological applications, including neurorehabilitation, which aims to promote neuroplasticity through active training. However, current iVR-based methods are constrained by the lack of an effective method to monitor brain activity during iVR. Most studies rely on a pre- vs. post-training paradigm, where the effectiveness of the therapy is assessed after the completion of one or several therapy sessions by comparing the post-intervention brain functions to the baseline.

To address this limitation, our ongoing research explores the feasibility of combining iVR with a flexible, non-invasive optical brain imaging method to monitor the brain responses to iVR-based tasks in real-time. Specifically, we will utilize functional Near-Infrared Spectroscopy (fNIRS), which employs near-infrared light to measure the cortical hemodynamic/oxygenation activities. Sharing a similar neurological basis as functional Magnetic Resonance Imaging (fMRI), fNIRS provides unique advantages in its portability, relatively higher resilience to motion, and cost-effectiveness, making it particularly suitable for iVR applications [2].

In Section 2, we present the methods used to develop an integrated iVR-fNIRS platform, detailing the experimental setup and the procedures for monitoring brain activity during hand-grasping tasks in different environments. Section 3 outlines the results of our preliminary analysis, including signal quality, brain activation patterns, and functional connectivity during different experimental conditions. In Section 4, we discuss the implications of our findings, highlighting the potential of iVR-based neurorehabilitation and the need for further investigation. Finally, Section 5 concludes the paper by summarizing the research and proposing future work, including the integration of haptic feedback into the iVR-fNIRS platform for enhanced therapeutic outcomes.

II. METHODS

We developed an integrated iVR-fNIRS platform capable of reliably measuring brain oxygenation changes during iVR (Figure 1). The platform combines an HTC Vive Pro VR headset (HTC Corp., New Taipei, Taiwan) with a multichannel fNIRS system (Rogue Research Inc., Montreal, Canada), allowing us to monitor brain activity during immersive virtual tasks. To test the platform, we designed an iVR-based training task centered on hand grasping, a commonly used activity in upper extremity rehabilitation due to its role in improving motor and executive control functions [3].

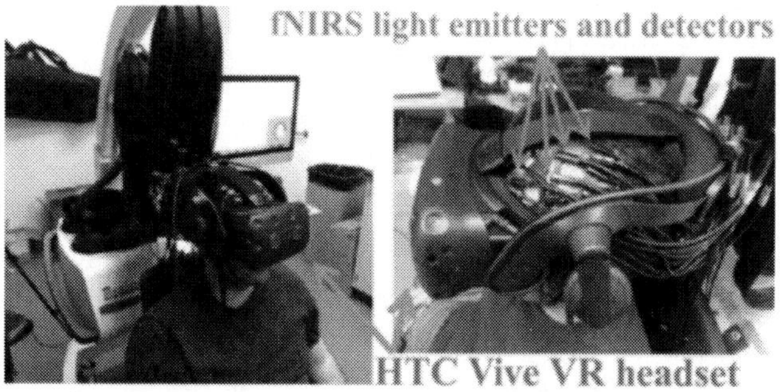

Figure 1: Test setup with commercial VR headset and multichannel fNIRS for real-time assessment of brain condition during VR.

We plan to recruit 30 healthy volunteers to participate in this study. For each participant, three data acquisition sessions will be conducted, with the same tasks presented (1) in the real-world environment, (2) in a non-immersive environment (computer screen), and (3) in the fully immersive VR environment (Figure 2). The order of sessions will be randomized to ensure the accuracy and reliability of the test. The same task will be performed 8 times within one session, while fNIRS will be used to continuously measure the brain responses to the hand-grasping task from the Bilateral Motor Cortices (M1) and the Dorso-Lateral Pre-Frontal Cortices (DLPFC).

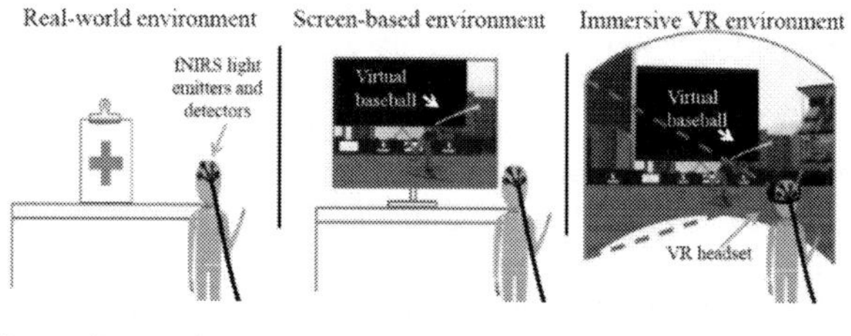

Figure 2: Hand grasping task in three environments: A real-world environment, a non-immersive VR environment, and an Immersive VR environment.

Participants will be invited to sit comfortably in a chair. (1) In the real-world environment session, a clipboard will be installed in front of them, displaying green or red cross indicators to signal the start or stop of tasks, respectively. The data acquisition session will last approximately six minutes, and involves 8 tasks of motor execution, where participants lift their right forearm and open and close their right hand according to the green or red indicator to mimic a baseball-catching motion. (2) In the computer screen environment, they will sit on a chair while a virtual baseball player avatar is displayed on a screen in front of them. The same data acquisition session will take place, where they will execute the ball-catching actions in response to the avatar's virtual baseball throws. (3) In the fully immersive VR environment (Figure 3), a VR headset will be installed on the participant's head together with the fNIRS light emitters and detectors, which will simulate a VR baseball field and a virtual player throwing a baseball at them (Figure 3). The same motor execution tasks will be performed, where they will open and close their right hand to complete the ball-catching actions in response to the virtual baseball being thrown at them. The VR game was developed using the Unity engine (Unity Technologies, San Francisco, United States).

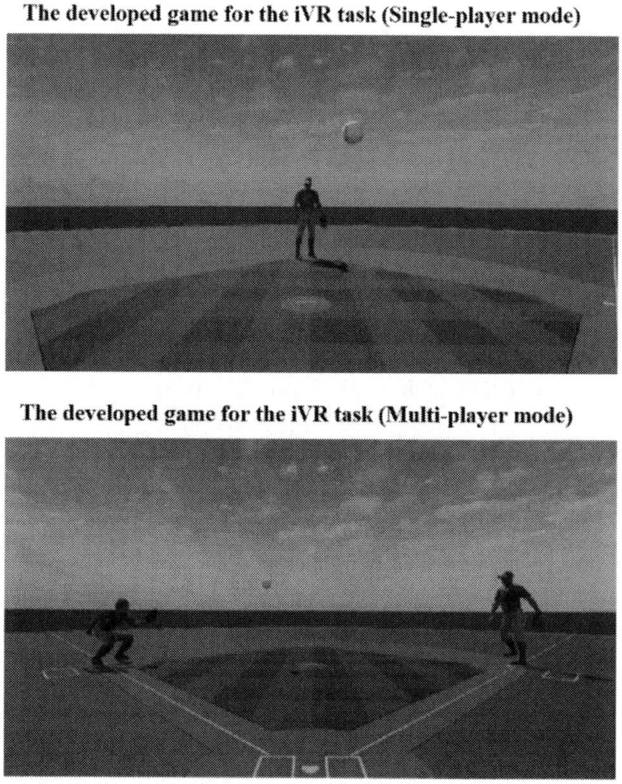

Figure 3: Hand grasping task in immersive VR environments: the single-player mode (interactive) and the multi-player mode (observatory).

A total of 10 fNIRS light emitters and 24 light detectors will be used in this study, forming 36 normal channels of 3cm to sample signals from the M1 and the DLPFC of both hemispheres (Figure 4). Six short-distance detectors will also be placed at approximately 1cm from the nearest light emitter to provide an estimation of the extracerebral signal components, such as the interferences from heart rate or blood pressure changes. fNIRS data will be sampled at 25Hz. In Figure 4, red and blue dots indicate light emitters and light detectors, respectively. Black dots represent the short-distance detectors. Yellow lines show the location of the formed fNIRS channels.

fNIRS data will be processed using the open-source Matlab toolbox Homer2 [4]. Briefly, the optical intensity time course will be converted to optical density changes. Band-pass filtering will be performed to limit the frequency range from 0.01Hz to 0.5Hz, removing components that are unlikely to have a neurological basis. The filtered optical density changes will be transformed into oxy-hemoglobin (HbO) and de-oxy hemoglobin (HbR) concentration changes using the modified Beer-Lambert law. The Hemodynamic Response Function (HRF) to the hand-grasping task in different environments will be estimated through the use of a general linear model, which will include short-distance fNIRS measurements to remove the physiological interferences.

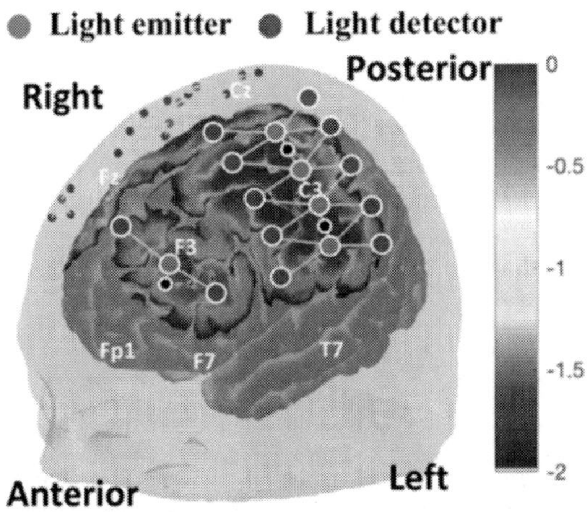

Figure 4: Depiction of the fNIRS channel setup used in this study.

We will also use beta-series correlation methods [5] to examine differences in the functional connectivity within and between the M1 and DLPFC to evaluate the impact of iVR on brain network functions [6].

III. RESULTS

To date, we have collected and analyzed data from two healthy volunteers (one female). Preliminary results showed no significant signal interference between the two devices and high signal-to-noise ratios (~32 ± 13 dB) in fNIRS recordings during the iVR sessions. These results suggest that the fNIRS system provided reliable and accurate data under immersive VR conditions. In all the environments, fNIRS revealed HbO increases and HbR decreases in the bilateral M1 and DLPFC cortices during hand-grasping tasks (Figure 5).

Comparing iVR-based tasks with the real-world and the screen-based tasks, we observed higher levels of HbO increase and lower HbR response, indicating greater neural activation during iVR compared to both the real-world environment and the computer screen-based non-immersive environment (Table 1). These findings highlight potentially enhanced neural engagement and functional activation that occur during immersive virtual tasks.

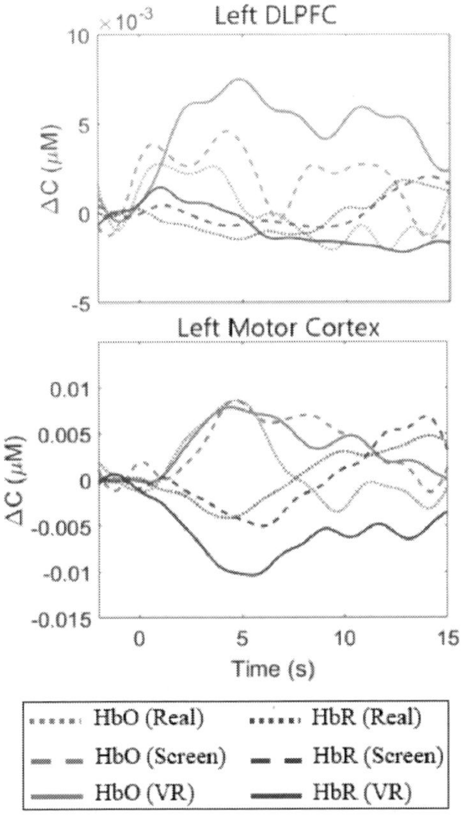

Figure 5: The HRFs of HbO and HbR concentration changes to motor tasks. Top: Left DLPFC; Bottom: Left M1. Overall, fNIRS revealed the highest levels of brain activities during iVR.

TABLE I: QUANTITATIVE COMPARISON BETWEEN HBO AND HBR LEVEL IN DIFFERENT ENVIRONMENTS. HBO AND HBR LEVELS WERE MEASURED IN BOTH DLPFC AND MOTOR CORTEX.

	Average HbO (μM)	Min HbO (μM)	Max HbO (μM)
DLPFC - iVR	0.0044551	-0.00044723	0.0074947
DLPFC - Screen	0.0018198	-0.0014499	0.0045801
DLPFC - Real	0.0011403	-0.0010942	0.0037368
Motor Cortex - iVR	0.0060339	-0.00039013	0.012586
Motor Cortex - Screen	0.004392	-0.00080191	0.010561
Motor Cortex - Real	0.0038074	-0.0010547	0.012893

	Average HbR (μM)	Min HbR (μM)	Max HbR (μM)
DLPFC - iVR	-0.00076602	-0.0022027	0.001435
DLPFC - Screen	0.000083154	-0.00082238	0.0020052
DLPFC - Real	-0.00097372	-0.0023726	0.0002035
Motor Cortex - iVR	-0.00053821	-0.01034	0.00054269
Motor Cortex - Screen	-0.0059486	-0.0054591	0.0064086
Motor Cortex - Real	-0.0019377	-0.0065365	0.00020121

In addition to the HRF analyses, we estimated the functional connectivity between each pair of fNIRS channels, and observed more co-functioning brain areas and stronger remote network connections, especially between M1 and DLPFC, which are both key regions in the executive control network, during tasks executed in the fully immersive VR environment (Figure 6).

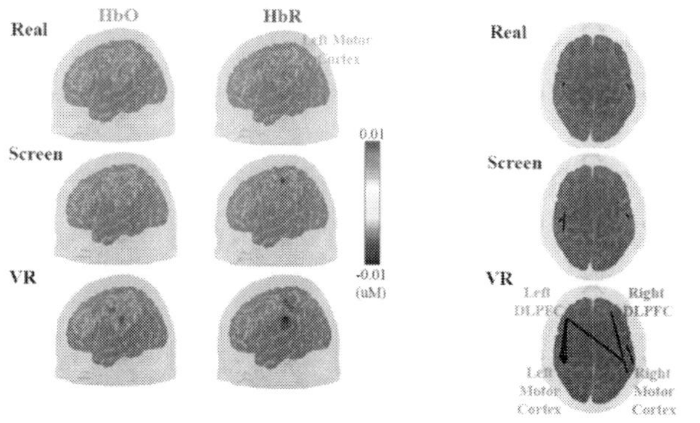

Figure 6: Connectivity analysis showed more connected brain areas during iVR task than the other environments, *p<0.05*, false discovery rate-corrected.

These results imply greater engagement of motor and cognitive control functions during iVR-based tasks.

IV. Discussion

The integration of iVR and fNIRS presents exciting opportunities for advancing neuroscience research and clinical applications. In this study, we developed an iVR-fNIRS platform that ensures optimized hardware compatibility and real-time data transmission. Preliminary findings demonstrate the potential of this combined platform in investigating motor and cognitive control functions during iVR-based tasks.

It is important to note that none of the experimental conditions (real-world, non-immersive VR, or immersive VR) incorporated tactile sensory feedback, such as interacting with a real ball. This decision aligns with the primary aim of our research: to design a neurorehabilitation approach that is accessible for diverse environments, beyond traditional hospital or rehabilitation center settings. Despite the absence of haptic feedback, our results suggest that iVR-based neurorehabilitation can potentially enhance brain activity and connectivity—a critical goal in neurorehabilitation aimed at fostering more effective and efficient brain stimulation.

Furthermore, the findings indicate that the iVR environment may offer a greater rehabilitative effect compared to real-world or non-immersive VR settings. This underscores the potential value of iVR as a platform for neurorehabilitation and warrants further investigation into its applications. Looking ahead, we plan to incorporate haptic feedback into the platform and examine its influence on the outcomes of our experiments. By doing so, we aim to explore whether the addition of tactile sensory input further enhances the rehabilitative effects observed in the iVR environment.

V. Conclusion and Future Work

Combining iVR and fNIRS provides an effective method to evaluate brain activity and function in a fully-immersive virtual environment. In this ongoing study, our preliminary data showed higher levels of brain activation and connections during iVR-based tasks compared with real-world environment, or computer screen-based non-immersive environment. With the integration of AI into the iVR-fNIRS platform, we offer significant potential to enhance the personalization and effectiveness of rehabilitation programs. AI-driven algorithms can be used to analyze large datasets of brain activity in real-time, leading to identifying patterns in neural responses that may not be immediately apparent to human researchers. For instance, machine learning models could be trained on brain activity data collected during iVR-based tasks, enabling the platform to adaptively modify the difficulty and nature of rehabilitation exercises based on individual performance and neural engagement. Furthermore, AI could facilitate the creation of personalized rehabilitation protocols by predicting optimal tasks or interventions tailored to each participant's cognitive and motor abilities, thus improving rehabilitation outcomes. By integrating these AI-driven models, the platform could offer dynamic and adaptive therapeutic programs that evolve with the patient's progress, making neurorehabilitation more efficient and targeted. As data collection continues, this research has the potential to lay the groundwork for innovative tools in neuroscience and neurorehabilitation, including facilitating immediate evaluation of iVR-based training efficacy and enabling the development of advanced, AI-driven personalized rehabilitation programs for both physical and cognitive recovery.

References

[1] C. J. Bohil, B. Alicea, and F. A. Biocca, "Virtual reality in neuroscience research and therapy," *Nature Reviews Neuroscience*, vol. 12, no. 12, pp. 752–762, 2011. DOI: 10.1038/nrn3127.

[2] K. Peng *et al.*, "iVR-fNIRS: Studying brain functions in a fully immersive virtual environment," *Neurophotonics*, vol. 11, no. 2, p. 020601, 2024. DOI: 10.1117/1.NPh.11.2.020601.

[3] F. Coupar, A. Pollock, L. A. Legg, C. Sackley, and P. van Vliet, "Home-based therapy programmes for upper limb functional recovery following stroke," *Cochrane Database of Systematic Reviews*, vol. 2012, no. 5, pp. 1–36, 2012. DOI: 10.1002/14651858.CD006755.pub2.

[4] T. J. Huppert, S. G. Diamond, M. A. Franceschini, and D. A. Boas, "Homer: A review of time-series analysis methods for near-infrared spectroscopy of the brain," *Applied Optics*, vol. 48, no. 16, pp. D280–D298, 2009. DOI: 10.1364/AO.48.00D280.

[5] K. D. Karunakaran *et al.*, "Can pain under anesthesia be measured? pain-related brain function using functional near-infrared spectroscopy during knee surgery," *Neurophotonics*, vol. 10, no. 2, p. 025014, 2023. DOI: 10.1117/1.NPh.10.2.025014.

[6] L. Gagnon *et al.*, "Short separation channel location impacts the performance of short channel regression in nirs," *NeuroImage*, vol. 59, no. 3, pp. 2518–2528, 2012. DOI: 10.1016/j.neuroimage.2011.08.095.

Towards Personalized Mobility Assessment and Rehabilitation: A User Centered Designed VR/XR-Based Solution for Older Adults

Yann Morère
University of Lorraine
LCOMS, EA 7306
Metz, France
email: yann.morere@univ-lorraine.fr

Jérôme Dinet
University of Lorraine
2LPN, UR 7489
Nancy, France
email:jerome.dinet@univ-lorraine.fr

Fabien Clanché
University of Lorraine
UFR STAPS
Nancy, France
email: fabien.clanche@univ-lorraine.fr

Thierry Bastogne
University of Lorraine
CRAN, UMR 7039
Nancy, France
email: thierry.bastogne@univ-lorraine.fr

Matthieu Casteran
University of Lorraine
2LPN, UR 7489 - DEVAH, UR 3450
Nancy, France
email: matthieu.casteran@univ-lorraine.fr

Lucas Detto
University of Lorraine
LCOMS, EA 7306
Metz, France
email: lucas.detto@univ-lorraine.fr

Matthieu Burtin
Mist Studio
Nancy, France
email: matthieu.burtin@miststudio.fr

Frédéric Bousefsaf
University of Lorraine
LCOMS, EA 7306
Metz, France
email: frederic.bousefsaf@univ-lorraine.fr

Kaoutar El Ghabi
University of Lorraine
LCOMS, EA 7306
Metz, France
email: kaoutar.elghabi@univ-lorraine.fr

***Abstract*—This paper presents our project addressing mobility loss in older individuals, funded by the MAIF Foundation for research. *Background:* During the aging process, the prevalence of falls can be mitigated by maintaining mobility as much as possible. Mobility, regardless of age, is a key factor in leading an active and independent life. Aging, by limiting certain abilities, gradually leads to a reduction in mobility. *Method:* In this societal context of generalized population aging, our consortium of researchers and companies aims to develop three interconnected actions to: Accurately evaluate the cognitive-motor performance of older individuals; Stimulate the development of physical and mental skills through motivational exercises; Monitor older individuals in their homes to intervene as early as possible in their care pathways. Our methodology leverages the expertise of the consortium to develop innovative methods serving patients, caregivers, and health professionals to preserve motor, cognitive, and attentional skills, contributing to slowing down senescence. Our working hypothesis is to act early by evaluating and attempting to slow mobility loss. *Results:* User-centered design is at the core of our project. In this paper, we focus on a design phase of a serious game aimed at determining the most relevant avatars and virtual environments (game atmosphere) for our older patient audience. A total of 35 participants were recruited and divided into 7 focus groups of 5 people. To best determine the type of avatar and environment that would suit our target population, we define two independent variables: the avatar and the theme of the environment. They are represented by visual examples, which in our case are presented in five different modalities. At the end of the interviews and after processing the collected data, the analysis of the dependant variables is made showing a categorization according to the participants' preferences.**

Keywords-Virtual and augmented reality; mobility of the older; evaluation; remobilisation; movement activity assesment; focus group.

I. Introduction

Today, individuals over 60 years old represent a quarter of the population and could account for one-third by 2050. Although life expectancy after age 50 in France is the highest in the EU, the number of healthy years lived remains lower than in several other countries [1]. This suggests a projected increase in the number of dependent older individuals, rising from 1.2 million in 2012 to 2.3 million by 2060 [2]. Preventing falls and the loss of autonomy is, therefore, a critical challenge for the coming decade.

Indeed, falls are the leading cause of accidents among individuals over 65 years old. In France, approximately one-quarter of people aged 65 to 85 report experiencing a fall each year, and the frequency of such incidents increases with age [3]. Falls result from a multifactorial interplay of risk factors, including mobility, age, comorbidities, gender, and educational level [4][5]. Their consequences can be severe for affected older individuals, leading to fractures, hospitalizations, loss of autonomy, and even institutionalization. To mitigate this risk, nearly one-fifth of individuals aged 55 to 85 report limiting their movements due to a fear of falling [6].

To address this significant public health issue, various therapeutic approaches have been developed. Multifactorial interventions can reduce the risk of falls by approximately 30% [7].

During the aging process, the prevalence of falls can be mitigated by encouraging mobility in older adults as much as possible. Mobility, regardless of age, is a critical factor for maintaining an active and autonomous life. However, aging, through the gradual limitation of certain capabilities, tends to lead to a progressive decline in mobility.

In regard to the definition of mobility, as formulated by the World Health Organization (WHO) in 2001, the International Classification of Functioning and Disability (ICF) is conceptualized as a universal framework focused on the description of how people live with a health condition [8][9][10]. Three levels of human functioning are classified: 1) body functions and structures as physiological and psychological functions, as well as body impairments, and anatomical deficiencies; 2) limitations in performing tasks or actions; and 3) participation restrictions in daily-life. In [9], functional mobility is defined as the manner in which people are able to move around in the environment in order to participate in the activities of daily living and, move from place to place. Movements include standing, bending, walking and climbing. Functional mobility provides opportunities for a person to engage in physical activities at home, school and in the community thereby contributing to health related quality of life. In our research context, an activity can be defined as the execution of a task or action by an individual, such as walking and the stability required for functional mobility. This phenomenon, influenced by both individual and social factors, results in significant variability among individuals. Consequently, it is not feasible to define a standard level of mobility based solely on a specific age.

Recent studies have highlighted a significant reduction of over 50% in the "life radius" for individuals over 75 years of age. According to these studies, difficulties with walking account for only 2% of mobility challenges, despite walking constituting 40% of the primary mode of movement within this age group [11].

Given the variability in individual situations and the inevitable trend of reduced mobility capacities with aging, it appears crucial to propose a coordinated and personalized approach. Such an approach would involve evaluating mobility, engaging individuals in playful re-mobilization activities, and validating the outcomes through longitudinal monitoring.

In section II, we will describe the final goal of our project, the section III will present the scientific context and the tools used to implement our solutions. The section IV presents a preliminary study concerning the design phase of a serious game aimed at determining the most relevant avatars and virtual environments (game atmosphere) for our older patient audience through focus groups. Finally the section V concludes the communication.

II. Assessment of Mobility

In this broader societal context of an aging population, extended life expectancy, and the aim of maintaining health, mobility in older adults has emerged as a significant concern. According to [12], outdoor mobility is a prerequisite for "aging well," impacting both physical and mental well-being by fostering social exchanges, activities, interactions, and social cohesion [13].

Currently, assessment tools are often limited to evaluation scales like AGGIR, ADL, IADL, WHOQOL-BREF, and EuroQol-5-Dimension. From a technical perspective, the literature features numerous studies on gait analysis in older adults using sensors [14], biomechanical studies employing multi-sensor data fusion [15], and the use of IMU sensors for gait analysis [16]. For instance, Anikwe et al. [17] demonstrates the critical role of mobile health monitoring systems in human health, while Torku et al. [18] present a user-centered approach employing wearable sensors to collect physiological signals and location data. Virtual Reality (VR) and Augmented Reality (AR) have also been explored in studies on older adults' quality of life, though their applications in healthcare contexts remain limited [19]. This study [20] focuses on the effect of immersion in a virtual scenario on mobility during the aging process. Older people exhibited a more reduced locomotor performance in a virtual environment than young adults, thereby their functional mobility score decreased more to complete the task, reflecting the adoption of a more secure locomotion strategy often related to the fear of falling, with an increase in time and number of steps to support balance.

VR and AR have also been explored in studies on older adults' quality of life, though their applications in healthcare contexts remain limited.

In [21], the authors explored the impact of the XR application focusing on exergames for rehabilitation. The paper presented the design rationale and development of an XR application. The evaluation of the system by ten senior users offered encouraging results. These highlighted that the combinatory approach of physical and virtual activities within an immersive and photorealistic VR environment offers an enticing and motivating approach to elder users to improve their physical well-being.

Despite these advances, few studies adopt a comprehensive approach to evaluating the mobility of aging individuals by considering their care journey, healthcare practitioners, and caregivers. Even rarer are those that integrate re-mobilization solutions, minimally invasive monitoring, and an assessment of the impact on quality of life.

Our working hypothesis is to take early action to assess and attempt to slow the decline in mobility. This concept is illustrated in Figure 1.

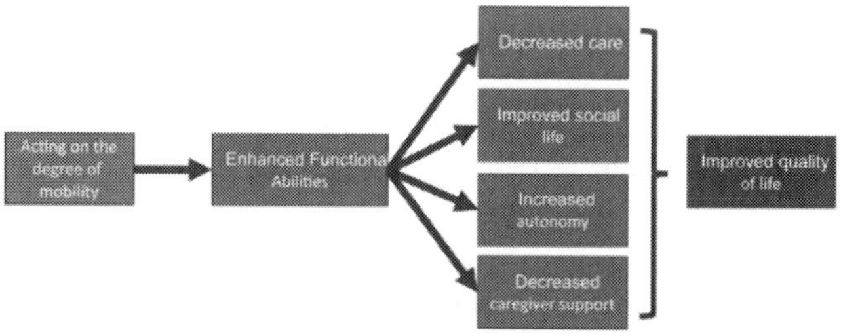

Figure 1. Expected societal impact.

Preserving motor, cognitive, and attentional abilities helps slow the aging process (senescence) [3]. To better evaluate mobility and offer tools for re-mobilization, our project proposes a technological solution for practitioners based on virtual and augmented reality. This solution is designed to collect and identify various mobility indicators, automate experimental protocols and data collection, ensure reproducibility of experimental conditions, and immerse patients in realistic environments and everyday life scenarios [22].

III. Materials and Methods

The following section presents the project's objectives as well as its innovative aspects. The tools and methods used are also introduced.

A. *Project Objectives*

The development of a stimulating digital tool, based on a gamified approach to physical exercise, aims to enable patients with limited mobility to maintain an appropriate level of physical activity for their upper and lower limbs. It is important to emphasize that rehabilitation in a healthcare center is not accessible to everyone; therefore, the tool should complement and/or extend current care programs.

However, motivational exercises performed independently by patients or older individuals require supervision and a method to assess their impact on the intensity of daily physical activities over a longer period to detect mobility changes. For example, Inertial Measurement Unit (IMU) sensors are increasingly being used to characterize human postures and movements [23][24].

By gathering this information, the identification of new mobility biomarkers should enable automated analysis of individual behavioral strategy evolution. This high-level information, shared among healthcare professionals, patients, and their companions, will enable the implementation of efficient actions throughout the care journey. The proposed solution should facilitate the implementation of coordinated actions. Figure 2 outlines the key objectives of our project.

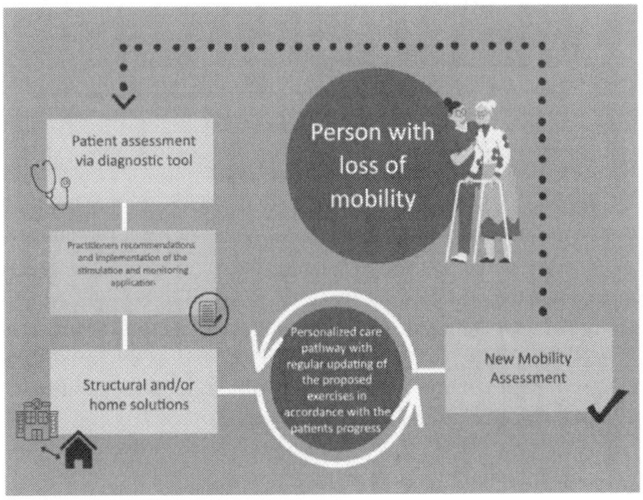

Figure 2. Objectives of the project.

Our technological contribution involves integrating virtual reality immersion technologies with eye-tracking, physiological signal, and movement measurement technologies. This enables us to quantify the cognitive-motor performance of older individuals during health examinations.

By identifying the underlying factors of mobility loss early on and offering a tailored remobilization path, we aim to improve the patient's mobility and reduce the risk of falls.

B. *Innovative Aspects*

Current tools for detecting fall risk often lack precision in prevention efforts. For instance, in [25] the authors reviewed 25 studies involving 2,314 subjects and found that a Timed Up and Go (TUG) test with a threshold of 13.5 seconds identified only 32% of individuals at risk of falling and yielded a negative result in 73% of subjects with no fall risk. Fall risk arises from numerous factors linked to the interaction between the patient and their environment. Attention, cognitive, or motor deficits, combined with environmental disturbances or distractions, can disrupt the motor control of a patient, potentially creating risky situations, as illustrated in Figure 3 [22].

To better address the multifactorial nature of fall risk, some test protocols assess motor abilities in scenarios that also involve manual or cognitive tasks [26]. It has been observed that incorporating a manual or cognitive task enhances the discriminative power of the TUG test.

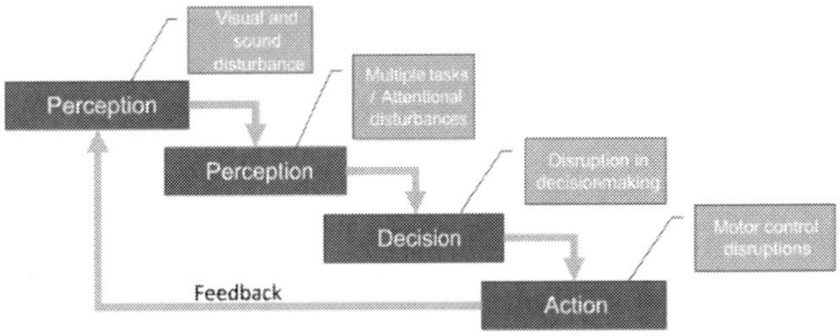

Figure 3. Motor control loop and its disturbances.

Environmental challenges faced by patients must be considered in fall risk assessments. For instance, tripping over obstacles is a major cause of falls [27]. Navigation around and over obstacles varies between younger and older individuals [28]. The height of the foot during obstacle crossing has been shown to predict fall risk [29]. Unlike the TUG test, these tests are challenging to implement in clinical settings as they often require specialized measurement equipment and post-processing of kinematic data.

To enhance diagnostic accuracy, we propose an experimental protocol informed by clinical practices and existing research protocols. This solution leverages VR and AR technologies combined with motion tracking sensors, eye-tracking devices, and physiological signal monitors to provide a comprehensive evaluation of a patient's condition during testing.

The experimental data acquired in a realistic environment will allow the assessment of motor, cognitive, and attentional capacities, as well as the emotional state of the patient. An integrated analysis of these data will define mobility indicators aimed at enhancing diagnostic accuracy. Participants will be immersed in a VR scenario, creating standardized audiovisual stimuli to measure motor responses to various perturbations. Motor responses will be captured using VR/AR system sensors, quantifying reaction times and adaptation strategies.

Unlike traditional methods, which rely on basic decision rules, our evaluation will initially use scientifically validated statistical techniques. Once a substantial dataset is collected, we will employ artificial intelligence (AI) techniques to construct predictive models of fall risk. This approach will enable healthcare personnel, even non-specialists, to perform fall risk diagnostics.

Our project aims to replace simplistic decision-making methods with advanced algorithms, providing a detailed and nuanced diagnostic prediction. This enhancement will help identify the optimal care pathways for patients. A critical step in this process involves defining interpretable biomarkers of fall risk that are easily understood by medical professionals. These biomarkers will serve as the foundation for creating precise and actionable prognostic tools.

C. *Tools*

To address these challenges, numerous clinical tests have been developed to assess patients' motor skills. We propose a tool leveraging virtual and augmented reality that implements tests inspired by existing literature, allowing for the evaluation of patients' motor, cognitive, and attentional capacities in an immersive, realistic environment.

For this project, we aim to develop three interconnected actions (see Figure 4):

- Precisely assess the cognitive-motor performance of older individuals;
- Stimulate the development of physical and mental skills through motivational exercises;
- Monitor older individuals at home to intervene as early as possible in their care pathway.

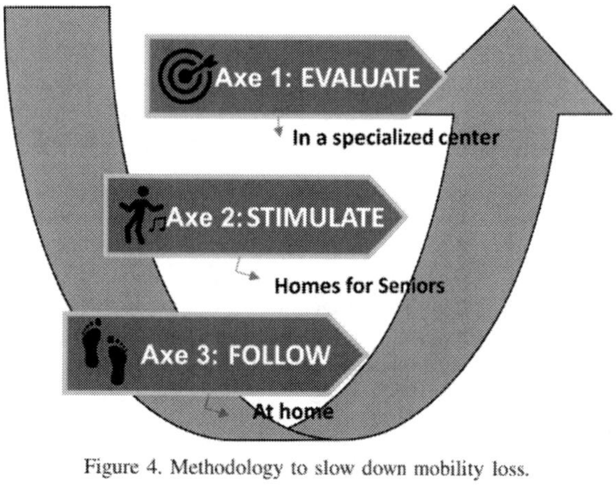

Figure 4. Methodology to slow down mobility loss.

Our methodology relies on the combined expertise of the project consortium to develop innovative methods that benefit patients, caregivers, and healthcare professionals.

User-centered design is at the core of our project. All methods and tools are selected in collaboration with the final users of our applications. To this end, we have involved two specialized partners in the project: OHS Lorraine (Office d'Hygiène Sociale de Lorraine http://ohs-solutions.fr/), and ONPA (Office Nancéien des Personnes Âgées https://onpa.net/). Both of which focus on enhancing the autonomy of individuals affected by aging.

A preliminary study [30] allowed us to identify acceptable and practical equipment for the target population based on the project's objectives. This study resulted in the design of a solution consisting of three specific development axes:

- Axis 1: Detailed Patient Assessment in VR/AR . This application focuses on conducting detailed mobility assessments using VR/AR. It incorporates various mobility tests, notably the Timed Up and Go (TUG) test, performed in an immersive virtual environment to simulate conditions closely resembling the patient's daily reality (see Figure 5). In addition to motion tracking for mobility characterization and gaze monitoring, specific physiological signals of the patient (e.g., AED, ECG) will be acquired through a non-invasive wireless system to enrich the evaluation. For instance, the detection of stress caused by fear of falling will be included. This test can be repeated as often as necessary, such as after a physiotherapy regimen or when home monitoring signals a significant decline in mobility.

Figure 5. Mobility assessment in Virtual environment (Axis 1)

- Axis 2: Patient Remobilization through VR and AR Exergames. This immersive re-training application in VR/AR enables healthcare practitioners to design a personalized "virtual prescription" comprising a list of exercises tailored for the patient to perform using the application (see Figure 6). At the end of each session, the practitioner will receive a detailed summary of the patient's activities, allowing comparison with previous sessions. This feedback loop ensures continuous monitoring and adaptation of the rehabilitation plan based on the patient's progress.
- Axis 3: Patient Mobility Monitoring in Autonomy. This application interfaces with an inertial measurement unit (IMU) carried by the patient during their daily activities at home (see Figure 7). The system continuously tracks the patient's mobility, capturing detailed data on their movement patterns and behavioral strategies within their living environment. By analyzing these patterns, healthcare providers can monitor changes in mobility, identify early

Figure 6. Graphic Universe of VR/AR Remobilization Exercises (Axis 2).

signs of functional decline, and intervene promptly with appropriate therapeutic strategies. The goal of this axis is to complement clinical assessments with real-world, day-to-day mobility data, offering a comprehensive understanding of the patient's condition and enabling personalized care plans.

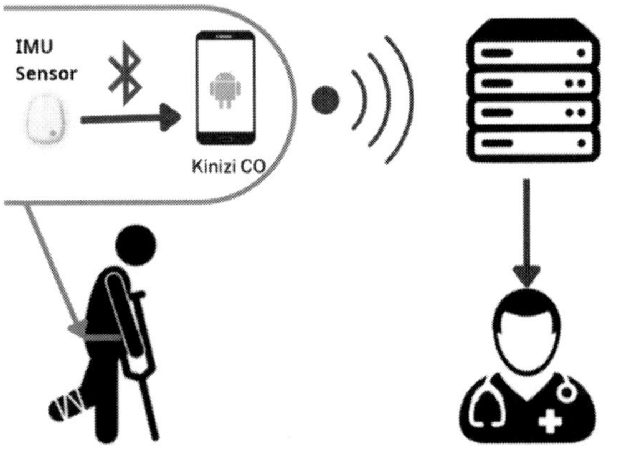

Figure 7. Home mobility monitoring (Axis 3).

D. Materials and Software

Depending on the different axes of the project, various materials will be used, ranging from the most complex acquisition systems (Axis 1) to the simplest and lightest ones for monitoring (Axis 3), and a gamified virtual/augmented reality remobilization system for Axis 2.

For Axis 1, the following materials have been selected (cf. Figure 8):

- HTC XR Elite headset, as it features a passthrough system allowing it to be used in both VR and AR. It also includes eye-tracking through an optional module. Its API enables natural hand interaction without the need for joysticks.
- In addition, HTC Ultimate trackers and Wrist trackers will be used due to their high accuracy [31][32] for tracking the trunk and limb positions during user activities.
- Physiological signals from the person will be recorded using a TEA Captiv [33] system with wireless, minimally invasive sensors.
- The entire evaluation application is developed using Unity for the real-time serious gaming part and Blender for modeling. The various HTC and TEA APIs are interfaced in C# with Unity.

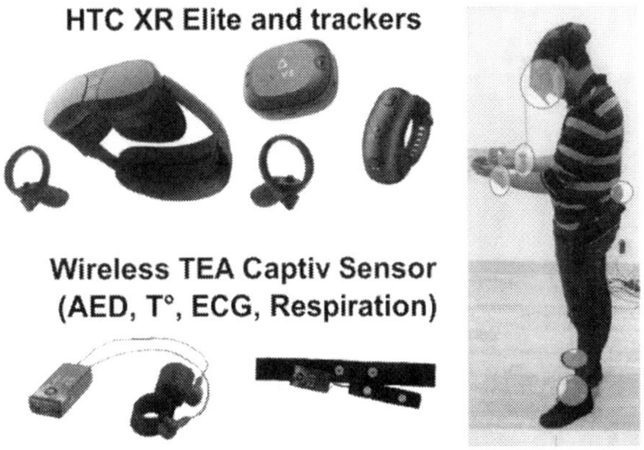

Figure 8. Axe 1 devices: HTC XR Elite and TEA wireless sensors.

For Axis 2, our partner Mist Studio [34] has selected the Meta Quest 3 VR/AR headset (cf. Figure 9). This state-of-the-art headset offers excellent technical specifications and is easy to use. A first gamified exercise is currently under development, and the results section will address the choice of avatars and the theme of the serious game environments by analyzing the opinions and attitudes of older people *a priori* through a study conducted using focus groups.

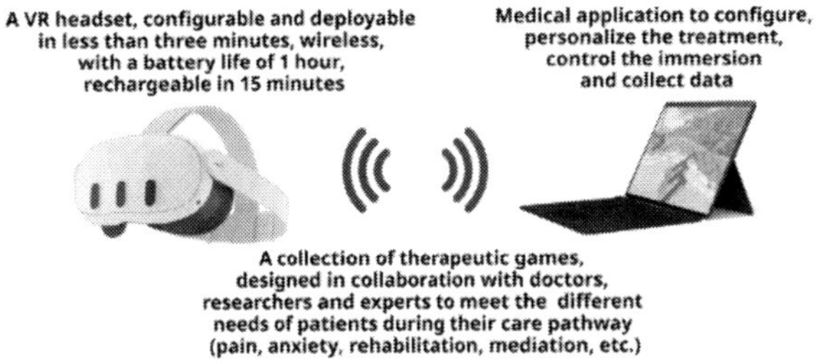

Figure 9. Axe 2 devices : Meta QUest 3 and dedicated applications.

Axis 3 focuses on the longitudinal monitoring of users' mobility. To achieve this, our partner Cybernano [35] conducted a study to select an Inertial Measurement Unit (IMU) sensor that meets user requirements identified in the study [30], as well as technical requirements such as weight, sensor storage capacity, battery life, and Bluetooth data download speed to the smartphone. After conducting an experimental study to compare several products on the market, the MetaMorionR sensor from MBIENTLAB was chosen. At 11 grams, it satisfies all the required criteria.

This sensor is integrated into a complete information transfer ecosystem. A Proof of Concept (POC) has been developed using the architecture shown in Figure 10. To implement this part of the project, a mobile application (named KINIZI), a web application (also named KINIZI), and a library (named libkinizi-playground), which serves as the foundation for applications using sensors to collect data, have been developed. The next step is to conduct real-world testing.

Security requirements related to data storage were considered during the architecture design. However, the device will be classified as "Wellness" rather than "Medical Device" to avoid costly certifications for the startup Cybernano.

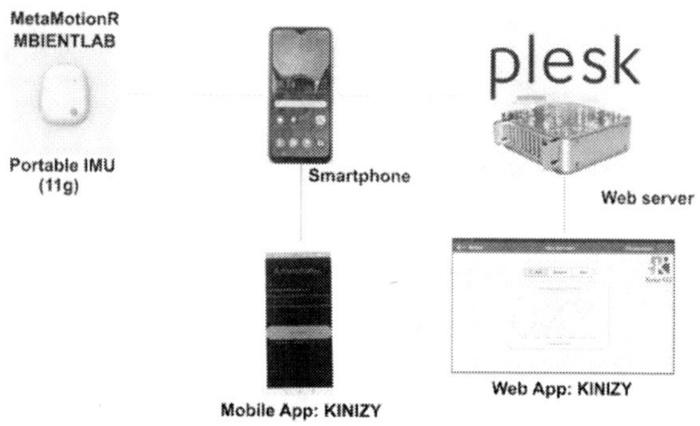

Figure 10. Axe 3 devices : MetaMotionR IMU and data acquisition architecture.

The final part of this communication focuses on the user-centered study that helps determine the most relevant avatars and environments for our older patient audience in the context of Axis 2: exergames for remobilization.

In this phase of the project, we aim to gather insights from older adults to identify avatars and virtual environments that resonate with them. This will ensure that the exergame is not only motivating but also relatable and enjoyable. To achieve this, a study using focus groups was conducted to better understand the preferences, opinions, and attitudes of older adults regarding the design of avatars and environments in exergames. This feedback will be essential to create a more engaging and personalized experience for users, which is crucial for ensuring long-term participation and effectiveness in physical rehabilitation.

This approach is rooted in the broader trend of "user-centered design," which prioritizes the needs, abilities, and preferences of the end-user—in this case, older adults—in order to create a more effective and user-friendly tool. The goal is to make the exercise more accessible and motivating for users, helping them stay engaged with their rehabilitation while providing measurable benefits for their mobility and overall health.

IV. User oriented avatars and environments design

This preliminary study focuses on the application of virtual/augmented reality remobilization in Axis 2. It consists in the design phase of a serious game aimed at determining the most relevant avatars and virtual environments (game atmosphere) for our older patient audience.

The representation of humans in virtual reality as avatars is a complex task because it is influenced by several factors such as the "Proteus effect" [36][37][38][39] and the Uncanny Valley [40].

The "Proteus effect" means that the avatar is not just a simple costume but a "full and complete self-representation" that enables two processes [41]: *deindividuation*, which is the alteration of self-awareness and the ability to critically assess one's actions, and *rationalization*, which means that individuals influence their own attitudes and behaviors in the virtual environment in line with the identity cues conveyed by the avatar. The Uncanny Valley, on the other hand, is the discomfort felt when avatars or robots appear "too close" to human but not quite human-like enough [42]. However, according to a more recent study [43], this phenomenon seems to be less pronounced among older people.

To define the avatars and environments for the exergame, a study was conducted through interviews with the target population using focus groups.

A. Participants

A total of 35 participants were recruited and divided into 7 focus groups of 5 people. The average age was 73.2 years with a standard deviation of 5.7 years. The youngest participant was 68.3 years old, and the oldest was 82.1 years old. The study included a majority of women (29 out of 35 participants, or 82.8%). The educational levels were distributed as follows: pre-Baccalaureate (82.8%), Baccalaureate (8.5%), and post-Baccalaureate (8.7%).

B. Protocol

The protocol for a focus group interview session is described in Figure 11.

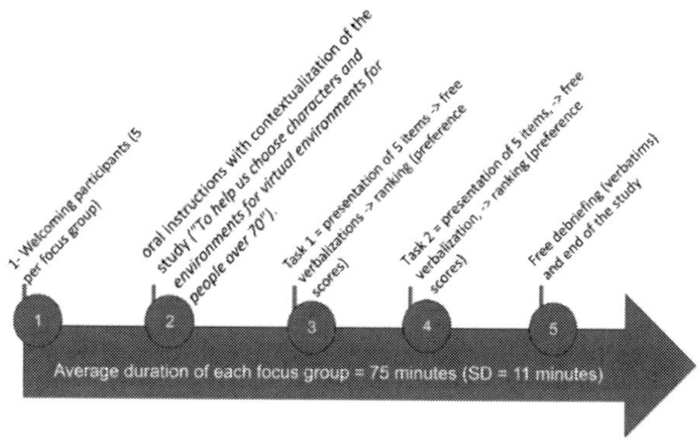

Figure 11. Focus group protocol

C. Method

To best determine the type of avatar and environment that would suit our target population, we define two independent variables (IVs), which are the factors manipulated during the study: the avatar (IV1) and the theme of the environment (IV2).

These independent variables are represented by visual examples, which in our case are presented in five different modalities (cf. Figure 12).

We then define the dependent variables (DVs) that will serve as our measures: a preference score from 0 to 10 (DV1), and the frequencies and occurrences of the adjectives and nouns produced during the interview (DV2).

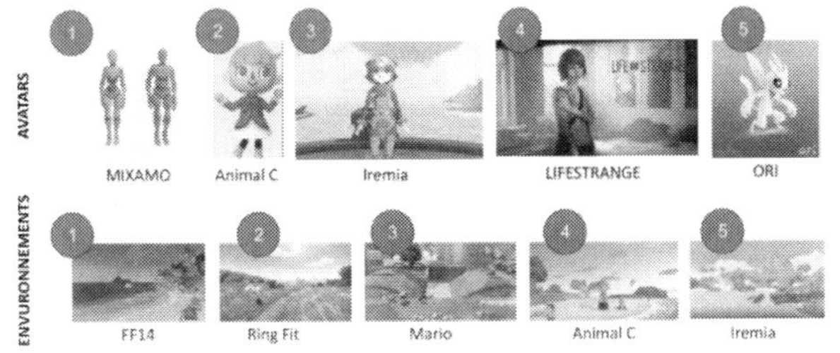

Figure 12. Independent variables : Avatars and environment

The overall analysis plan (AP) is given by the following relationship.:

$$AP = S_{35} \times IV1_5 \times IV2_5$$

We also formulate several control variables to avoid biasing the experience:

1) Counterbalancing of items for each task (to avoid an order effect);
2) Counterbalancing of the two tasks (to avoid an order effect);
3) The same avatars and environments are presented;
4) "Limited" experience with digital environments (online games, smartphone games);
5) No severe cognitive impairments;
6) The same facilitator for all focus groups;
7) Avatars and environments are presented according to a number (to avoid vocabulary effects);
8) Use of the same video projector (1800 lumens);
9) Same projection size (75-inch screen);
10) Same distance between participants and the screen;
11) No known or proven speech disorders;
12) Correct vision declared (correction for 80% of participants);
13) Data collection during the month of July 2024.

D. Results

At the end of the interviews and after processing the collected data, the analysis of the VD1 variable (preference score, see Figure 13) clearly shows a strong preference for three avatars (3, 2, and 4), with a notable disappointment for avatars 5 and 1. There is also a significant difference between the two categories (4 vs 5, $p < .001$). However, it is worth noting that there are individual differences, likely due to the Proteus effect.

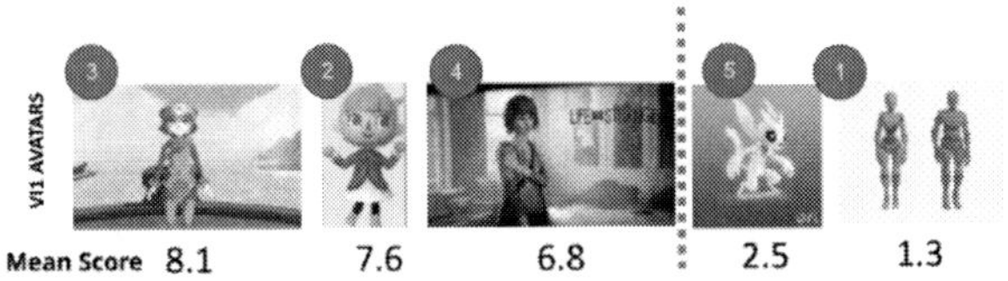

Figure 13. Results : preference score for avatars

Similarly, we analyze the variable IV2 related to environments (see Figure 14). A clear preference is observed for environments 5, 2, and 1 in terms of average scores. Opinions are more reserved for the last two environments, 4 and 3. As with variable IV1, a significant difference is observed between the two categories 1 and 4 ($p < .001$). On this variable, fewer inter-individual differences are noted, with many significant positive correlations (see table I).

Some additional remarks can be issued from the Table 1:

- There is a negative and significant correlation between opinions for avatars 1 and 5, the first one being very robot-like while the second being more "fun";
- There are positive and significant correlations between opinions about environments 1, 4 and 5. These three environments represent a beach in a very pleasant way;
- In the same way, there are positive and significant correlations between environments 3 and 4, and between environments 4 and 5 which represent "simple" and funny physical environments extracted from video-games;

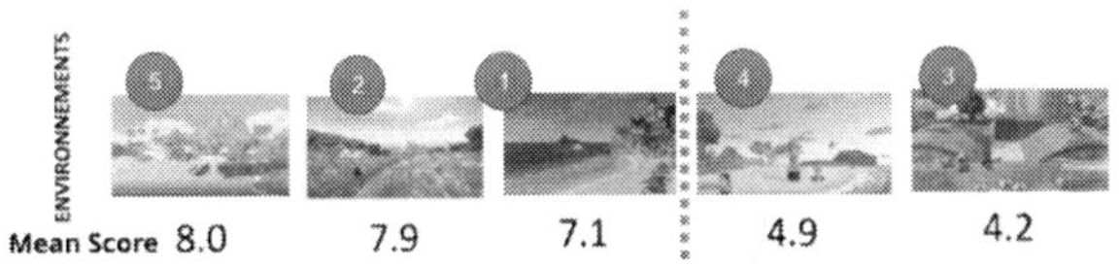

Figure 14. Results : preference score environments

Figures 15 and 16 display the results for the variable DV2: frequencies and occurrences of adjectives and nouns produced during the interviews for the independent variables Avatar and Environment.

These figures offer a detailed breakdown of how participants described the different avatars and environments, providing insight into their preferences and the associations they made with each option. By examining the frequency of terms, we gain a deeper understanding of the emotional and cognitive responses of the older participants toward various virtual representations and settings.

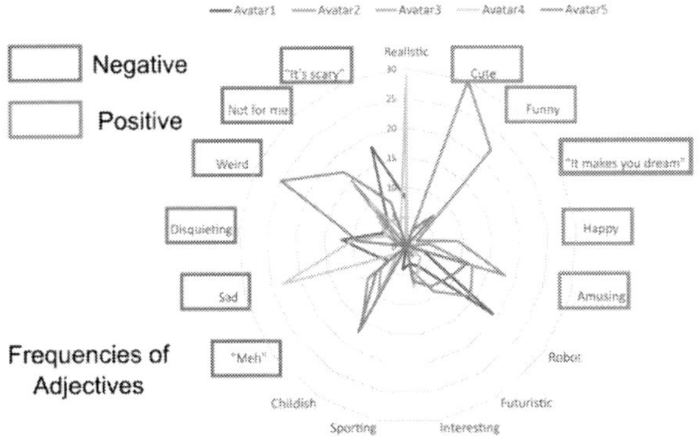

Figure 15. Results : frequencies and occurrences of adjectives and nouns for avatars

Adjectives with positive (green), negative (red) and neutral meanings can be classified.

The adjectives can be categorized as positive (in green), negative (in red), and neutral. This classification helps to further understand the participants' emotional and cognitive responses toward the avatars and environments they encountered during the interviews. Positive adjectives reflect favorable perceptions,

TABLE I. GENERAL CORRELATION MATRIX

		Avat.1	Avat.2	Avat.3	Avat.4	Avat.5	Env.1	Env.2	Env.3	Env.4	Env.5
Avat.1	Pearson's r	–	×	×	×	×	×	×	×	×	×
	p-value	–	×	×	×	×	×	×	×	×	×
Avat.2	Pearson's r	0.203	–	×	×	×	×	×	×	×	×
	p-value	0.243	–	×	×	×	×	×	×	×	×
Avat.3	Pearson's r	0.132	0.260	–	×	×	×	×	×	×	×
	p-value	0.451	0.132	–	×	×	×	×	×	×	×
Avat.4	Pearson's r	0.007	0.408 *	0.105	–	×	×	×	×	×	×
	p-value	0.967	0.015	0.548	–	×	×	×	×	×	×
Avat.5	Pearson's r	-0.526 **	0.194	-0.176	0.209	–	×	×	×	×	×
	p-value	0.001	0.263	0.312	0.229	–	×	×	×	×	×
Env.1	Pearson's r	0.002	-0.309	0.011	-0.283	-0.064	–	×	×	×	×
	p-value	0.992	0.070	0.950	0.099	0.715	–	×	×	×	×
Env.2	Pearson's r	-0.004	-0.211	-0.105	-0.105	-0.033	0.925***	–	×	×	×
	p-value	0.983	0.224	0.547	0.550	0.846	<0.001	–	×	×	×
Env.3	Pearson's r	-0.082	0.140	-0.039	0.031	0.025	0.040	-0.029	–	×	×
	p-value	0.642	0.423	0.822	0.860	0.888	0.818	0.867	–	×	×
Env.4	Pearson's r	-0.070	-0.153	0.133	-0.339*	-0.051	0.577***	0.334*	0.694***	–	×
	p-value	0.691	0.380	0.447	0.047	0.773	<0.001	0.05	<0.001	–	×
Env.5	Pearson's r	-0.52	-0.241	-0.035	-0.213	-0.038	0.945***	0***.936	0.103	0.539***	–
	p-value	0.768	0.164	0.840	0.220	0.828	<0.001	<0.001	0.555	<0.001	–

Note : $^{*}p < 0.05$, $^{**}p < 0.01$, $^{***}p < 0.001$

such as describing avatars as "friendly" or environments as "relaxing." Negative adjectives, on the other hand, indicate discomfort or dissatisfaction, like "unclear" or "strange." Neutral adjectives might indicate ambivalence or a lack of strong opinion, such as "ordinary" or "simple."

This categorization provides valuable insight into the participants' preferences and the overall emotional impact of the virtual elements used in the study. By analyzing these frequencies and occurrences, researchers can refine the avatars and environments to better suit the needs and expectations of older users.

As Figure 15 shows, participants produced more positive adjectives for two avatars (avatars 3 and 4, perceived as "cute", "funny", "happy", "amusing"). In the same way, as Figure 16 shows, participants produced more positive words for three environments (environments 1, 2 and 5, perceived as "calm", "funny", colorful", "paradisaical", "exotic").

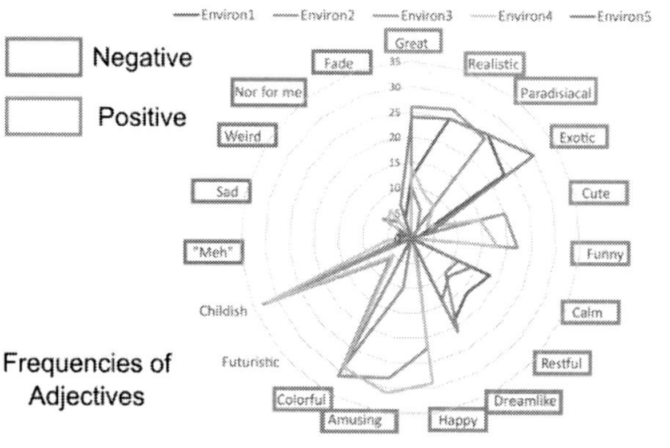

Figure 16. Results : frequencies and occurrences of adjectives and nouns for environments

These opinions and attitudes *a priori* allowed to highlight clear preferences for certain avatars and for certain environments (see Figure 13). Thanks to this study, we can conclude about the possible choices in terms of avatars and environments in line with our target population. The preferred combinations, i.e., the best combination according to the participants, are summarized in Figure 17.

Figure 17. Possible choices for avatars and environments

E. Discussion

Although the results were significant, a number of limitations emerged. The first concerns the static nature of the avatars and environments proposed. Participants would have liked to see avatars in action and made comments such as: "It doesn't move", "What can it do?", "It's weird, everything is frozen...".

As the precise context of use was not presented, the participants also asked the following questions : "But what is it for?", "Is it for playing games?

As in our previous study [30] the impact of personal experience is very important and can modify the study : "With my grandson, I sometimes play this thing", "I've already seen it on TV", "It looks like my granddaughter".

There was no objective assessment of our participants' sensitivity to colour and contrast, which led to comments such as: "I can't see anything at all", "What's that in the background, water or mountains?

We did not escape the uncontrolled group effects (majority influence, minority influence, leadership, etc.) which interfered with our study. This is reflected in phrases such as : "Well, if others think that, then...", "Would you use that later? Well, I'll be damned".

V. Conclusion

This paper gives an overview of our project to address the loss of mobility in the older. Using 3 axes of action: assessment, remobilization and follow-up, we aim to slow down the loss of mobility and thus ultimately increase quality of life. To achieve this, we will be developing technological tools based on virtual and augmented reality, as well as longitudinal mobility monitoring using sensors worn by the patient. The general principles of these 3 development axes were described. The second part of the presentation focused on the development method used, which constantly puts the end-user at the heart of the development process, making him or her an active participant in the choices made. Thanks to a focus group method, we were able to determine the most relevant avatars and virtual environments (game atmosphere) for our older patient audience. These highlights will be incorporated into new virtual and augmented reality scenarios to assess and improve the mobility of the older. Ultimately, this solution could help in the care of the older by providing healthcare professionals with a precise and effective tool for assessing and monitoring changes in mobility. The next stages of the research involve extending the tests to a larger sample and developing more advanced rehabilitation functions, in order to confirm the results obtained and assess the long-term impact of this approach on the quality of life of the older.

Acknowledgement

This project is supported by grants issued from Fondation MAIF (Mutuelle d'assurance automobile des instituteurs de France https://www.fondation-maif.fr)

References

[1] "Healthy Life Expectancy in France - Working Papers - Ined Editions", Ined - Institut national d'études démographiques, Accessed: Mar. 10, 2025. [Online]. Available: https://www.ined.fr/fr/publications/editions/document-travail/esperances-vie-incapacite-france.

[2] "Aging well - santé publique france", Accessed: Mar. 10, 2025. [Online]. Available: https://www.santepubliquefrance.fr/la-sante-a-tout-age/la-sante-a-tout-age/bien-vieillir.

[3] "Activité physique et prévention des chutes chez les personnes âgées · Inserm, La science pour la santé", Inserm, Section: Expertises collectives, Accessed: Mar. 10, 2025. [Online]. Available: https://www.inserm.fr/expertise-collective/activite-physique-et-prevention-chutes-chez-personnes-agees/.

[4] J. A. Painter and S. J. Elliott, "Influence of gender on falls", *Physical & Occupational Therapy in Geriatrics*, vol. 27, no. 6, pp. 387–404, 2009.

[5] J. T. Hanlon, L. R. Landerman, G. G. Fillenbaum, and S. Studenski, "Falls in african american and white community-dwelling elderly residents", *The Journals of Gerontology Series A: Biological Sciences and Medical Sciences*, vol. 57, no. 7, pp. M473–M478, 2002.

[6] C. Léon and F. Beck, "Les comportements de santé des 55-85 ans", *Analyses du Baromètre santé*, vol. 194, 2010.

[7] M. E. Tinetti, C. F. M. De Leon, J. T. Doucette, and D. I. Baker, "Fear of falling and fall-related efficacy in relationship to functioning among community-living elders", *Journal of gerontology*, vol. 49, no. 3, pp. M140–M147, 1994.

[8] M. Leonardi *et al.*, "Icf in neurology: Functioning and disability in patients with migraine, myasthenia gravis and parkinson's disease", *Disability and rehabilitation*, vol. 31, no. sup1, S88–S99, 2009.

[9] M. Forhan and S. V. Gill, "Obesity, functional mobility and quality of life", *Best practice & research Clinical endocrinology & metabolism*, vol. 27, no. 2, pp. 129–137, 2013.

[10] W. H. Organization *et al.*, "Towards a common language for functioning, disability, and health: Icf", *The international classification of functioning, disability and health*, 2002.

[11] N. Benlahrech, A. L. Ruyet, C. Livebardon, and M. Dejeammes, "The Mobility of Elderly People: Analysis of Household Travel Surveys", Pages: 54 pages, figures, graphiques, tableaux, bibliographie pages 52 à 54, report, Centre d'études sur les réseaux, les transports, l'urbanisme et les constructions publiques (CERTU), 2001.

[12] "Study on senior mobility in france - inclusive mobility", Accessed: Mar. 10, 2025. [Online]. Available: https://www.mobiliteinclusive.com/etude-seniors/.

[13] F. Huguenin-Richard, A. Dommes, M.-A. Granié, M.-S. Cloutier, and C. Coquelet, *Walking among elderly people: Mobility and safety challenges*, 2014.

[14] L. Ruiz-Ruiz, A. R. Jimenez, G. Garcia-Villamil, and F. Seco, "Detecting fall risk and frailty in elders with inertial motion sensors: A survey of significant gait parameters", *Sensors*, vol. 21, no. 20, p. 6918, 2021, Publisher: MDPI.

[15] V. Bijalwan, V. B. Semwal, and T. Mandal, "Fusion of multi-sensor-based biomechanical gait analysis using vision and wearable sensor", *IEEE Sensors Journal*, vol. 21, no. 13, pp. 14 213–14 220, 2021, Publisher: IEEE.

[16] I. Mulas *et al.*, "C linical assessment of gait and functional mobility in italian healthy and cognitively impaired older persons using wearable inertial sensors", *Aging clinical and experimental research*, vol. 33, pp. 1853–1864, 2021, Publisher: Springer.

[17] C. V. Anikwe *et al.*, "Mobile and wearable sensors for data-driven health monitoring system: State-of-the-art and future prospect", *Expert Systems with Applications*, vol. 202, p. 117 362, 2022, Publisher: Elsevier.

[18] A. Torku, A. P. Chan, E. H. Yung, J. Seo, and M. F. Antwi-Afari, "Wearable sensing and mining of the informativeness of older adults' physiological, behavioral, and cognitive responses to detect demanding environmental conditions", *Environment and Behavior*, vol. 54, no. 6, pp. 1005–1057, 2022, Publisher: Sage Publications Sage CA: Los Angeles, CA.

[19] R. S. Baragash, H. Aldowah, and S. Ghazal, "Virtual and augmented reality applications to improve older adults' quality of life: A systematic mapping review and future directions", *Digital health*, vol. 8, p. 20 552 076 221 132 099, 2022, Publisher: SAGE Publications Sage UK: London, England.

[20] A. Renaux, F. Clanché, F. Muhla, *et al.*, "Age-related decrease in functional mobility score when performing a locomotor task in an immersive environment", *Frontiers in Bioengineering and Biotechnology*, vol. 11, 2023, ISSN: 2296-4185. DOI: 10.3389/fbioe.2023.1141507.

[21] V. Charissis, S. Khan, S. AlTarteer, and R. Lagoo, "Virtual rehabilitation: Xr design for senior users in immersive exergame environments", in *2024 IEEE Gaming, Entertainment, and Media Conference (GEM)*, 2024, pp. 1–6. DOI: 10.1109/GEM61861.2024.10585464.

[22] F. Clanché *et al.*, "Virtual reality as assessment tool of the risk of falls in the elderly", *International Journal of Sensors and Sensor Networks*, vol. 11, no. 1, pp. 11–17, Jun. 2023, Number: 1 Publisher: Science Publishing Group, ISSN: 2329-1788. DOI: 10.11648/j.ijssn.20231101.12.

[23] D. L. Marques *et al.*, "An experimental study on the validity and reliability of a smartphone application to acquire temporal

variables during the single sit-to-stand test with older adults", *Sensors (Basel, Switzerland)*, vol. 21, no. 6, p. 2050, Mar. 15, 2021, ISSN: 1424-8220. DOI: 10.3390/s21062050.

[24] J. Zhou *et al.*, "A novel smartphone app-based assessment of standing postural control: Demonstration of reliability and sensitivity to aging and task constraints", in *2020 IEEE International Conference on E-health Networking, Application & Services (HEALTHCOM)*, Mar. 2021, pp. 1–6. DOI: 10.1109/HEALTHCOM49281.2021.9398972.

[25] E. Barry, R. Galvin, C. Keogh, F. Horgan, and T. Fahey, "Is the timed up and go test a useful predictor of risk of falls in community dwelling older adults: A systematic review and meta-analysis", *BMC geriatrics*, vol. 14, pp. 1–14, 2014.

[26] R. C. Vance, D. G. Healy, R. Galvin, and H. P. French, "Dual tasking with the timed "up & go" test improves detection of risk of falls in people with parkinson disease", *Physical therapy*, vol. 95, no. 1, pp. 95–102, 2015, Publisher: Oxford University Press.

[27] S. N. Robinovitch *et al.*, "Video capture of the circumstances of falls in elderly people residing in long-term care: An observational study", *The lancet*, vol. 381, no. 9860, pp. 47–54, 2013, Publisher: Elsevier.

[28] M. J. D. Caetano *et al.*, "Age-related changes in gait adaptability in response to unpredictable obstacles and stepping targets", *Gait & posture*, vol. 46, pp. 35–41, 2016, Publisher: Elsevier.

[29] D. T. Lai, S. B. Taylor, and R. K. Begg, "Prediction of foot clearance parameters as a precursor to forecasting the risk of tripping and falling", *Human movement science*, vol. 31, no. 2, pp. 271–283, 2012, Publisher: Elsevier.

[30] J. Dinet *et al.*, "Breaking social isolation for older people living alone with technology", *Behaviour & Information Technology*, vol. 43, no. 9, pp. 1740–1751, 2024. DOI: 10.1080/0144929X.2023.2298706. eprint: https://doi.org/10.1080/0144929X.2023.2298706.

[31] S. Merker, S. Pastel, D. Bürger, A. Schwadtke, and K. Witte, "Measurement accuracy of the htc vive tracker 3.0 compared to vicon system for generating valid positional feedback in virtual reality", *Sensors*, vol. 23, no. 17, p. 7371, 2023.

[32] J. Kulozik and N. Jarrassé, "Evaluating the precision of the htc vive ultimate tracker with robotic and human movements under varied environmental conditions", *arXiv preprint arXiv:2409.01947*, 2024.

[33] "Tea ergo", Accessed: Mar. 28, 2025. [Online]. Available: https://www.teaergo.com/fr/.

[34] "Mist studio", Accessed: Mar. 28, 2025. [Online]. Available: https://www.miststudio.fr/.

[35] "Cybernano", Accessed: Mar. 28, 2025. [Online]. Available: https://cybernano.eu/fr/accueil/.

[36] A. Ortiz *et al.*, "Elderly users in ambient intelligence: Does an avatar improve the interaction?", in *Universal Access in Ambient Intelligence Environments: 9th ERCIM Workshop on User Interfaces for All, Königswinter, Germany, September 27-28, 2006. Revised Papers*, Springer, 2007, pp. 99–114.

[37] M. V. Birk, C. Atkins, J. T. Bowey, and R. L. Mandryk, "Fostering intrinsic motivation through avatar identification in digital games", in *Proceedings of the 2016 CHI conference on human factors in computing systems*, 2016, pp. 2982–2995.

[38] A. Puri, S. Baker, T. N. Hoang, and R. C. Zuffi, "To be (me) or not to be? photorealistic avatars and older adults", in *Proceedings of the 29th Australian conference on computer-human interaction*, 2017, pp. 503–507.

[39] S. Baker *et al.*, "Avatar-mediated communication in social vr: An in-depth exploration of older adult interaction in an emerging communication platform", in *Proceedings of the 2021 CHI conference on human factors in computing systems*, 2021, pp. 1–13.

[40] J.-H. Tammy Lin and D.-Y. Wu, "Exercising with embodied young avatars: How young vs. older avatars in virtual reality affect perceived exertion and physical activity among male and female elderly individuals", *Frontiers in psychology*, vol. 12, p. 693 545, 2021.

[41] J. Guegan, S. Buisine, and J. Collange, "Effet proteus et amorçage: Ces avatars qui nous influencent", *Bulletin de psychologie*, vol. 547, no. 1, pp. 3–16, 2017.

[42] J. Dinet and R. Vivian, "Exploratory investigation of attitudes towards assistive robots for future users", *Le travail humain*, vol. 77, no. 2, pp. 105–125, 2014.

[43] Y.-C. Tu, S.-E. Chien, Y.-Y. Lai, J.-C. Liu, and S.-L. Yeh, "The uncanny valley revisited: Age-related difference and the effect of function type", *Innovation in Aging*, vol. 3, no. Supplement_1, S330–S330, 2019.

Enhancing the Utilization of Artificial Intelligence and Social Robots in Specialized Units for Children with Autism

Marie Rychalski
University of Lorraine
University of Lorraine - Association J.B Thiery
Nancy, France
email:marie.rychalski@univ-lorraine.fr

Armand Manukyan
University of Lorraine
Association J.B. Thiery - University of Lorraine
Nancy, France
email:Armand.MANUKYAN@jbthiery.asso.fr

Jérôme Dinet
University of Lorraine
2LPN, UR 7489, Chair BEHAVIOUR
Nancy, France
email:jerome.dinet@univ-lorraine.fr

***Abstract*—In France, approximately 700,000 individuals are affected by Autism Spectrum Disorders (ASD), including 100,000 children. ASD is primarily characterized by challenges in social interaction and communication, as well as restricted and repetitive behaviors. Recent technological advances, particularly in robotics, offer new opportunities to enhance social skills interventions for children with autism. Programs such as Treatment and Education of Autistic and related Communication Handicapped Children (TEACCH) and Early Intensive Behavior Intervention (EIBI) have proven effective in promoting communication, adaptive behaviors, and inclusion in mainstream settings. This ongoing study examines how educational teams perceive and integrate social robots into specialized classrooms for children with ASD. Three robots (NAO, Leka, and Buddy) were introduced in two specialized teaching units, with a focus on teacher and health professional acceptance and perceived utility. Data were collected through focus group discussions, Karasek's Job Strain Model questionnaire (decision latitude, psychological demands, and social support), the Self-Efficacy Scale (SES), and The Human–Robot Interaction Evaluation Scale (HRIES). The results indicate that higher decision latitude is positively associated with teachers' sense of self-efficacy. Perceptions of the robots varied significantly: Leka received the highest ratings for sociability and the lowest for disturbance, while NAO and Buddy elicited higher disturbance scores. Focus group discussions revealed several constraints—organizational, communicational, and institutional—that influence the successful adoption of robots. While participants acknowledged the potential of robotic tools to boost motivation and increase student engagement, they also expressed concerns regarding time investment, over-reliance on technology, and reduced human interaction. In conclusion, the findings emphasize the importance of careful planning and the creation of supportive work environments for the integration of social robots. Future research should focus on refining robot design, developing comprehensive staff training, and exploring larger-scale implementations to maximize learning outcomes for children with ASD.**

Keywords-autism; robots; artificial; intelligence; interactions; ergonomics.

I. INTRODUCTION

This section will introduce the subject of ASD and care to follow by the benefits of social robots for autistic people.

A. Autism and Care

In France, approximately 700,000 individuals are affected by Autism Spectrum Disorders (ASD), including 100,000 children. As outlined in the Diagnostic and Statistical Manual of Mental Disorders (DSM-5) and International Classification of Diseases (ICD-11), deficits in social interaction and communication are core characteristics of autism. People with autism are a highly heterogeneous group, making it difficult to pinpoint specific defining symptoms. The rapid advancements in technology, particularly in robotics, present significant opportunities for innovation in the treatment of individuals with ASD. Recent developments have enabled robots to perform a variety of human-like functions, offering potential to enhance social skills in individuals with ASD. Autistic children often struggle with social interactions and cooperation. They may appear uncooperative because they haven't yet learned the appropriate behaviors for different social situations, or they may have difficulty managing strong emotions, such as anger, frustration, or anxiety.

Recommendations for providing quality support to children with autism emphasize a multidisciplinary and intensive approach. Recent advances have enabled robots to perform a variety of human-like functions, offering valuable assistance in improving the social skills of individuals with ASD [1] [2] [3]. The process of teaching young learners with ASD is complex and multidimensional, involving numerous cognitive decisions made by educators before, during, and after instruction. This ongoing work examines educator cognition across the broader field of education, with a specific focus on the use of robots in special education settings. To date, research has primarily examined cognitive processes involved in planning, instruction, and reflection separately, often in controlled environments. It is recommended that future research adopt mixed methodologies, such as case studies, to explore educators' thoughts and actions holistically and within natural teaching environments. This would allow researchers to connect actual behaviors with the cognitive processes that underlie them.

ASD is characterized by two key criteria: first, a persistent deficit in social communication and interaction across multiple contexts, and second, restricted and repetitive patterns of behavior, interests, and activities. Children with ASD face challenges in adapting to their environment, including emotional, cognitive, and behavioral difficulties that can impact school learning. They may also struggle to respond to sensory stimuli in their environment [4].

B. Education and Interventions in Autism

The Treatment and Education of Autistic and related Communication Handicapped Children (TEACCH) approach is an educational program designed to support children with ASD and communication difficulties [5]. This method focuses on promoting self-determination and autonomy through the use of structuring strategies. It is applied across various contexts (such as school, work, and family) to improve skills like social behavior, communication, and learning, while also promoting inclusion in everyday settings. TEACCH employs time and space structuring, visual cues, task repetition, and individualized, structured interventions.

Some authors emphasize that TEACCH is a suitable program for the development of children with autism. [6] indicates that children with ASD who participate in Early Intensive Behavior Intervention (EIBI) generally outperform those receiving other treatments or standard care in terms of IQ and adaptive behavior measures. Sensory processing disorders in individuals with autism are characterized by altered perceptions of sensory stimuli. These changes can lead to hypo- or hypersensitivity across various sensory channels. Examples of sensory-specific behaviors include seeking light or reflections, avoiding noise or touch, displaying rigidity, or resisting change. Such behaviors can trigger reactive responses, posing challenges in educational and pedagogical support. To address these issues, a significant reorganization of activities is often required, ensuring both variation and adaptation to individual sensory profiles. Although systematically evaluating sensory differences is essential, creating and arranging activities and spaces that meet these needs remains a considerable challenge for professionals. Conventional interventions often rely on numerous supports and materials, which can limit the efficiency of activities and hinder the child's ability to complete tasks.

C. Benefits of Social Robots for Autism

Robots are increasingly being integrated into human environments. From simple industrial tasks to administrative guidance, they are gradually being deployed across various sectors to assist humans. Their design is becoming more complex, evolving towards humanoid forms. In the field of support, robotic agents are being developed to interact and adapt to intricate mechanisms, such as imitation and emotional expression. These advancements present new opportunities for educational and pedagogical support for children with autism. One key advantage is the predictability of technology, which is simpler and reduces unnecessary sensory information compared to human interaction. Technology is deterministic and predictable. While it doesn't express emotions in the same way humans do, it can mimic them and produce controlled responses during interactions with children, boosting their confidence and self-esteem. Furthermore, repeated interactions provide an ideal environment for trial and error, which is invaluable for learning. Robotic agents can stimulate behaviors such as imitation, joint attention, communication initiation, and social interaction in children with autism.

Several studies have demonstrated that participants with ASD often perform better in Robotic Conditions (RC) than in Human Conditions (HC). [7] suggests that children with ASD, as well as typically developing (TD) children, tend to focus more on the administrator in Robotic Conditions than in Human Conditions. [8] found that autistic children use the same brain resources when interacting with artificial agents as TD children do when interacting with human agents. These findings point to several positive implications for using robots with children with ASD. As a result, there is a growing body of research aimed at exploring whether artificial agents represent a promising new approach for improving deficits in children with autism. Research on social robots has increased in recent years, with numerous studies highlighting the positive interest and benefits these robots can bring to the learning process for autistic children, as well as their potential for regulating cognitive difficulties and reducing stereotypical behaviors.

D. Acceptability of the New Generation of Social Robots by Educational and Pedagogical Professionals

Buddy© is an "emotional" robot whose greatest merit is its ability to improve the quality of life of users of all ages. It can be used by children, adults and the elderly alike. In particular, it can be used to create social links through its various devices, to offer educational activities in a playful way, and to look after the elderly. Equipped with various sensors and cameras, Buddy© features high-performance voice and visual recognition, making it easy to use and interact with. Buddy© also comes with a range of applications to make learning fun. For example, the *Buddy Emoi* application lets you work in different ways on emotions with Buddy© as a student or as a teacher. Buddy© also includes an application, *BuddyLab*, for programming and customizing compositions, sequences of actions or emotions. This is a very interesting option for the rest of our study. Indeed, it will be possible to program Buddy© to give instructions, and express one emotion visually and another audibly.

The integration of robots into the classroom is a subject that raises numerous questions. It has the potential to disrupt certain teaching practices and require additional effort on the part of teachers. The acceptability and adoption of educational robots are influenced not only by their perceived usefulness but also by teachers' ability to integrate these new technologies into their teaching practices. In fact, the form of the robot influences its acceptability, categorizing the object and affecting the intention to interact [9][10]. Furthermore, incorporating a playful dimension into the user experience has been identified as a beneficial factor for enhancing acceptability, whereas an overly affective design can compromise the object's credibility. For example, the Nao robot, despite its affective design, suffers from a lack of credibility, which can represent a challenge for retailers looking to project an innovative brand image.

David et al. [11] [12] highlight the impact of mental anthropomorphism on the acceptability of robots. In fact, attribution of mental states to a social robot has been shown to generate feelings of anxiety and strangeness, which can lead to a decline in acceptability. Conversely, the experience of a sense of control has been shown to encourage the attribution of mental states and the establishment of a connection with robots, thereby reducing reactance. The existing research in this area demonstrates that individuals who experience a sense of control are more inclined to attribute mental states to robots and to feel a greater sense of connection and similarity with machines. However, a perceived absence of control fosters a sense of distance between humans and robots, thus diminishing acceptability.

Spatola et al. [13] proposed a multicomponent evaluation of anthropomorphism in their article. This innovative approach focuses on four key aspects: sociability, agency, animacy, and disturbance. These dimensions significantly influence perceptions and attitudes toward robots, highlighting the importance of considering them in the development and implementation of educational robots. The attribution of human characteristics to robots—such as "sociability," "agency," "animacy," and "disturbance"—can enhance their acceptability by fostering familiarity and reducing perceived threats.

E. Objectives and Research Question

The main objective of this study is to investigate the impacts of the integration of different robotic tools into specialized teaching units (nursery and elementary), in natural settings, for children diagnosed with autism spectrum disorders. The work is being carried out in collaboration with educational and teaching professionals who work with these children. Our main research question is: What are the conditions required for the integration of artificial intelligence and social robots to be accepted by education and health professionals in specialized units for autistic children?

This paper is structured as follows. In Section 2, we describe the methodology, detailing the participant demographics, hypotheses examined, and materials employed in data collection. Section 3 presents the main results obtained from quantitative measures and qualitative discussions within focus groups. Section 4 discusses the implications of these findings, particularly focusing on psychosocial factors influencing the acceptance of robots, perceptions of robot anthropomorphism, and insights gathered from educators. Finally, in Section 5, we summarize the conclusions drawn from this study and outline directions for future research aimed at enhancing the integration and effectiveness of artificial intelligence and social robots in specialized autism education settings.

II. Method

Three different robots have been integrated and compared to determine which is best suited to the context of specialized classes, while respecting the usual working conditions of professionals and children. The focus group method is employed for each group, with each session lasting for a duration of one hour. The objective of this method is to facilitate a discussion concerning the participants' feelings of self-efficacy in the workplace, their stress levels, and their perceptions of digital technology, with a particular emphasis on robots. The discussion is initiated in a general context and subsequently continues through the utilisation of anonymised individual questionnaires, which are completed on an individual basis.

A. Participants

The present study sample comprised eight female (2 teachers and 6 educators), all over 18 and of French nationality. They are from the educational and teachings professionals from two specialised teaching units (nursery and elementary) of the Association Jean-Baptiste Thiéry, located in the East of France.

B. Hypotheses

In our study conducted in natural settings, we examined three hypotheses.

1) Decision Latitude–Workload Hypothesis: Professionals who experience higher decision-making latitude will be more inclined to adopt AI-driven social robots, even when these tools introduce additional tasks or complexities. Greater autonomy in planning and execution is hypothesized to buffer the perceived workload increase.

2) Self-Efficacy–Workload Hypothesis: Professionals with a strong sense of self-efficacy are expected to display more positive attitudes toward integrating AI-equipped social robots, as they perceive themselves capable of managing the extra workload and adapting new procedures in ASD interventions.

3) AI Functionality–Workload Trade-off Hypothesis: If the perceived benefits of the robot's AI capabilities (e.g., improved engagement, more targeted interventions) outweigh the added workload, professionals will exhibit higher acceptance and integration of social robots in specialized education settings.

C. Material

In the context of the focus group, a microphone is employed for the purpose of recording the conversation. The audio recording is anonymized and confidentialized, ensuring that only the participants have access to it. For this reason, the groups will be anonymized and named Group 1 and Group 2. The SWOT method (strengths, weaknesses, opportunities and threats) is utilized during the discussion of the difficulties encountered in the workplace. Furthermore, a table is compiled, detailing both the expectations and fears concerning the integration and utilization of robotic tools.

The Karasek test [14] is utilized to evaluate the stress levels experienced by the professionals, while their sense of self-efficacy is measured using the Self-Efficacy Scale (SES) [15]

[16]. To assess the degree of anthropomorphism of the various robots employed in conjunction with the educational teams, Spatola's HRIES scale [13] is employed. The statistics were made with Jamovi and R softwares.[17][18].

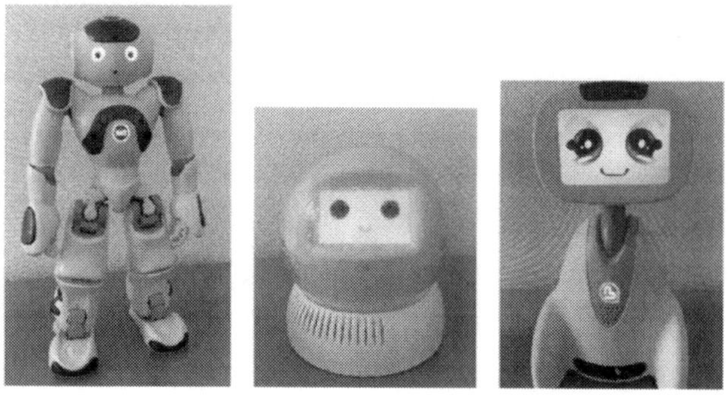

(a) (b) (c)

Figure 1. The three robots used in our study: NAO (a), Leka (b) and Buddy (c)

The robots NAO, Buddy, and Leka each offer complementary features, addressing specific goals in interaction, education, and mediation for children, particularly those with neurodevelopmental disorders. NAO, developed by SoftBank Robotics, is a sophisticated humanoid robot equipped with multiple sensors (tactile, sonar, inertial), HD cameras, multilingual voice recognition, and grasping capabilities, making it particularly suitable for teaching STEM subjects, providing assistance, or supporting educational activities. It can be programmed using interfaces like ZoraBot or AskNAO Tablet, which allow for highly customizable activities without requiring advanced technical skills. Buddy, created by Blue Frog Robotics, is a mobile, teleoperated robot on wheels, designed for intuitive interaction through a touchscreen, speech synthesis, and various sensors (infrared, touch, QR code). It serves as an emotional and educational companion, capable of displaying multimedia content and following programmed action sequences. Leka, on the other hand, stands out with its spherical, child-safe design and playful sensory features (LED lights, vibrations, sounds, movement) aimed at stimulating cognitive, emotional, and social development. Its intuitive software platform allows for easy adaptation to the individual needs of children, particularly in therapeutic contexts. Thus, NAO is positioned as a versatile, programmable tool for complex applications, Buddy as an interactive multimedia companion, and Leka as a sensory and educational device designed for mediation and stimulation of children with special needs. The professionals observe a demonstration of the robots in the classroom after the focus group. The discussion groups are convened in the respective classrooms of each group. Each participant is seated on a chair facing a table, with a distance of one meter maintained between each pair of participants. This configuration ensures sufficient visual privacy and facilitates effective interaction. Jamovi and R were used to analyse the results.

III. Main Results

Group 2 has a high degree of decision latitude, with an average of 80.5. Group 1 has lower decision latitude, with an average of 63.5. Both groups show moderate to high levels of psychological demand, with a combined mean of 22.75. Social support was rated as moderate to good, with an overall mean of 22.5.

TABLE I. DESCRIPTIVE STATISTICS OF ANTHROPOMORPHISM FACTORS FOR THE ROBOTS NAO, LEKA AND BUDDY USING THE HRIES SCALE [13].

Robots	Factors	Mean	Median	S-D	Minimum	Maximum
NAO	Sociability	2.46	2.46	1.817	1.180	3.75
	Animacy	2.41	2.41	1.549	1.310	3.50
	Agency	2.00	2.00	1.506	0.930	3.06
	Disturbance	3.12	3.12	0.707	2.620	3.62
Leka	Sociability	3.09	3.09	2.701	1.180	5.00
	Animacy	1.78	1.78	1.103	1.000	2.56
	Agency	2.00	2.00	1.414	1.000	3.00
	Disturbance	2.37	2.37	1.061	1.620	3.12
Buddy	Sociability	2.34	2.34	1.541	1.250	3.43
	Animacy	1.78	1.78	1.018	1.060	2.50
	Agency	1.81	1.81	1.237	0.930	2.68
	Disturbance	3.03	3.03	1.103	2.250	3.81

Pearson's correlation test revealed a moderate positive correlation between decision latitude and SES ($r = 0.78$, $p = 0.01$). The Pearson correlation test revealed a moderate non-significant correlation between social support and the robots' perceived sociability ($r = 0.49$, $p > 0.05$).

The Leka robot is perceived as very sociable with an average score of 3.09 and moderately disturbing with a score of 2.37. The NAO robot is considered very animated with a score of 2.41 but also very disturbing with a score of 3.12. The Buddy robot was considered very disturbing with a score of 3.03 and animated with a score of 1.78. The NAO and Buddy robots recorded the highest disturbance scores, 3.12 and 3.03 respectively.

Professionals in Group 2, with more decision-making latitude and better social support, perceived the robots more favourably, but reported higher levels of disturbance, especially for Buddy (3.81).

The focus groups identified the groups' vulnerabilities, including deficiencies in organisation, memory and rigour. Constraints revealed included transparency, professional cohesion and communication. External opportunities include interaction with diverse teachers, varied learning methods, training and supervision. External threats include lack of time, limited human resources, institutional constraints and bureaucracy.

The groups' expectations and fears centred on better understanding of the students, increased motivation, adoption of innovative tools, loss of time, dependence on technology and reduced social relations.

IV. Discussion

Data collected in natural settings allow to demonstrate several interesting findings.

A. Psychosocial Analysis

1) Psychosocial dimension (Karasek and SES questionnaires): The results of the decision latitude scores demonstrate a considerably elevated level of autonomy for group 2 (mean: 80.5) in comparison with group 1 (63.5). This heightened autonomy has the potential to result in enhanced job satisfaction and a more favorable perception of their abilities. Indeed, a moderate positive correlation ($r = 0.786$, $p = 0.010$) between decision latitude and SES demonstrates that professionals with greater autonomy in their work tend to have a more positive perception of their personal effectiveness.

With respect to the psychological demand dimension, both groups exhibit moderate to high levels, with a pooled average of 22.75. However, this pressure appears to be manageable for the majority of participants. The stress associated with high demands could increase the perception of disturbance generated by the robots, particularly NAO and Buddy, which record the highest disturbance scores (3.125 and 3.031, respectively).

The social support received is considered to be moderate to good (pooled mean: 22.5). This factor is closely linked to the positive perception of the robots, with a moderate non-significant correlation ($r = 0.493$, $p > 0.05$) between social support and the perceived sociability of the robots. Furthermore, it is observed that professionals benefiting from a favorable collegial environment appear more inclined to accept robots.

2) Perceptions of Robots (HRIES): The robots evaluated (Buddy, NAO, and Leka) demonstrate significant variation in terms of sociability, animation, and disruption. Leka is distinguished by its notably high sociability (mean: 3.094) and moderate disturbance (2.375), which leads to its emergence as the most popular robot. Conversely, NAO is regarded as the most animated (2.406) but also the most disruptive (3.125), which may impede its acceptance. Buddy, with balanced but lower scores, is perceived as neutral.

An intergroup comparison reveals that professionals in one of the two groups, who have greater decision-making latitude and better social support, perceive the robots more favorably. Conversely, these professionals report higher levels of disturbance, particularly in the case of Buddy (3.813).

3) Focus Group: A comprehensive analysis of the specialised units has revealed several pivotal aspects. The analysis has exposed inherent vulnerabilities within specific groups, manifesting as deficiencies in organisation, memory, and rigour. Conversely, other groups encounter constraints in terms of transparency, professional cohesion, and communication. An examination of external opportunities reveals that the groups benefit from interaction with a diverse range of teachers, varied learning methods, training, and supervision. The sharing of experiences and professional development stand out as significant assets. Conversely, these groups are confronted with external threats, including but not limited to: paucity of time, limitations in human resources, institutional constraints, unfamiliarity with management, timetabling constraints and bureaucracy. The expectations and fears of these groups centre on three key areas: improved understanding of pupils, heightened motivation and the adoption of innovative tools. However, these groups also express concerns regarding potential losses, including a loss of time, a dependence on technology and a diminution of social relations. This analysis underlines the multifaceted challenges and opportunities confronting special education groups, underscoring the necessity for a balanced approach to optimize benefits while mitigating risks.

V. Conclusion and Future Work

This study aims to explore the professional acceptance of AI-equipped social robots in specialized classrooms for children with autism, focusing on the interaction between decision latitude, self-efficacy, and the balance between perceived benefits and workload. The findings suggest that greater decision latitude helps offset the additional tasks associated with robot integration, while high self-efficacy promotes a more positive response to technology-induced challenges. Crucially, successful adoption depends on whether the educational advantages provided by the robots outweigh the time and resource investments required. Lessons learned from this study underscore the importance of organizational readiness, clear communication, and comprehensive initial training sessions. Failed attempts highlighted challenges such as robot-induced disturbances, and difficulties maintaining consistent engagement across diverse classroom contexts. The limitations of this study include a small sample size, limiting generalizability, and the specificity of the cultural and organizational contexts which may affect broader applicability. Technical limitations of the robots themselves, such as restricted adaptability and user-friendliness for non-specialist educators, also emerged as significant barriers. In conclusion, our analysis highlights the challenges and opportunities faced by special education groups, emphasizing the importance of a balanced approach to maximize benefits while mitigating risks. The integration of robots into these environments must be carefully planned to minimize perceived disruption and foster a collaborative, supportive work environment, ultimately enhancing interactions between children and professionals in autism therapy. The adoption of educational robots is influenced by numerous factors, including affective and social variables, robot design and configuration, and anthropomorphism. Future research should investigate these dimensions more precisely, focusing on technical enhancements such as adaptive algorithms for real-time behavioral analysis, machine learning-driven predictive engagement models, and modular robot designs. Additionally, future efforts should include larger-scale, multi-site studies and extensive educator training programs to improve usability and effectiveness, thereby better aligning educational robots with teachers' needs and expectations while minimizing potential resistance.

References

[1] H. Kumazaki *et al.*, "Optimal robot for intervention for individuals with autism spectrum disorders," *Psychiatry and clinical neurosciences*, vol. 74, no. 11, pp. 581–586, 2020.

[2] F. Papadopoulos, K. Dautenhahn, and W. C. Ho, "Exploring the use of robots as social mediators in a remote human-human collaborative communication experiment," *Paladyn*, vol. 3, pp. 1–10, 2012.

[3] B. Scassellati *et al.*, "Improving social skills in children with asd using a long-term, in-home social robot," *Science Robotics*, vol. 3, no. 21, eaat7544, 2018.

[4] L. Giacolini, P. Marti, and I. Iacono, "Game of stimuli: An exploratory tangible interface designed for autism," in *Proceedings of the European Conference on Cognitive Ergonomics 2015*, 2015, pp. 1–2.

[5] E. Schopler, G. B. Mesibov, R. H. Shigley, and A. Bashford, "Helping autistic children through their parents: The teacch model," in *The effects of autism on the family*, Springer, 1984, pp. 65–81.

[6] S. Panerai, L. Ferrante, and M. Zingale, "Benefits of the treatment and education of autistic and communication handicapped children (teacch) programme as compared with a non-specific approach," *Journal of intellectual disability research*, vol. 46, no. 4, pp. 318–327, 2002.

[7] E. Bekele *et al.*, "Understanding how adolescents with autism respond to facial expressions in virtual reality environments," *IEEE transactions on visualization and computer graphics*, vol. 19, no. 4, pp. 711–720, 2013.

[8] T. Chaminade *et al.*, "Fmri study of young adults with autism interacting with a humanoid robot," in *2012 IEEE RO-MAN: The 21st IEEE International Symposium on Robot and Human Interactive Communication*, IEEE, 2012, pp. 380–385.

[9] J. Lallement, S. Machat, F. Euzéby, and J. Passebois-Ducrot, "Do you think my robot is cute? understanding the determining factors of robot acceptability," in *32nd International Congress of the French Marketing Association*, 2016.

[10] J. Lallement, J. Ducros-Passebois, F. Euzéby, and S. Machat, "A fun robot, or nothing! what kind of robot in the service industry? questions on the determinants of human-robot interaction quality in commercial relationships," in *Funny Objects: A New Way of Making*, 2021.

[11] D. David, "Anthropomorphism as a strategy to compensate for a lack of control? the case of social robots and consequences on their acceptability," Ph.D. dissertation, Université Côte d'Azur, 2022.

[12] D. David, P. Thérouanne, and G. Schadron, "The feeling of control in the attribution of mental states and the acceptability of social robots," in *13th International Congress of Social Psychology, ADRIPS 2020*, 2020.

[13] N. Spatola, B. Kühnlenz, and G. Cheng, "Perception and evaluation in human–robot interaction: The human–robot interaction evaluation scale (hries)—a multicomponent approach of anthropomorphism," *International Journal of Social Robotics*, vol. 13, no. 7, pp. 1517–1539, 2021.

[14] R. A. Karasek Jr, "Job demands, job decision latitude, and mental strain: Implications for job redesign," *Administrative science quarterly*, pp. 285–308, 1979.

[15] A. Follenfant and T. Meyer, "Pratiques déclarées, sentiment d'avoir appris et auto-efficacité au travail. résultats de l'enquête quantitative par questionnaires," *Les apprentissages professionnels informels. Paris: L'Harmattan*, pp. 185–246, 2003.

[16] R. Schwarzer, "Generalized self-efficacy scale," *Measures in health psychology: A user's portfolio. Causal and control beliefs/Nfer-Nelson*, 1995.

[17] The jamovi project, *Jamovi*, Version 2.3 [Computer Software], 2022.

[18] R Core Team, *R: A language and environment for statistical computing*, R packages retrieved from MRAN snapshot 2022-01-01, 2021.

Ergonomic Challenges and Benefits of Enhanced Cultural Application with Augmented Reality for People with Autistic Spectrum Disorder

Ashe Maurice
University of Lorraine
Nancy, France
email: Ashe.Maurice6@etu.univ-lorraine.fr

Armand Manukyan
Association J.B. Thiery
Nancy, France
email: Armand.Manukyan@jbthiery.asso.fr

Antoine Pollet
University of Lorraine
Nancy, France
email: Antoine.Pollet@univ-lorraine.fr

Stéphanie Claudel
University of Lorraine
Nancy, France
email: Stephanie.Claudel@univ-lorraine.fr

Jérome Dinet
University of Lorraine
Nancy, France
email: Jerome.Dinet@univ-lorraine.fr

Laurent Dupont
University of Lorraine
Nancy, France
email: Laurent.Dupont@univ-lorraine.Fr

***Abstract*—Autism is a neurodevelopmental trouble which affects 1 child per 100 in the world. Known symptoms make museum exhibits difficult to access. The use of Augmented Reality (AR) (covering real environment with digital objects) by this population is growing rapidly but remains poorly documented, especially in the context of museum visits. AR used in this context often involves the use of a tablet and not a headset, as in the present experiment. 40 recruited participants will visit museums using augmented reality devices. The benefits of such a device will be assessed using an ergonomic evaluation grid. Psychometric tests will also be proposed to assess the cognitive cost of the protocol for the participants, alongside with observation and interviews. In this way, data about acceptability of the equipment, suitability of the software for our participants, relevance of the course and content of the application and about the behaviour induced by the AR device will be collected. This project aims to assess to which extent augmented reality can be implemented in the realization of a tour museum route by a participant with an autism spectrum disorder. This research will shed light on the advantages of using an augmented reality headset compared with a tablet, which has already been widely documented. In addition, a comparison between traditional visits and visits based on augmented reality will truly highlight the benefits of AR technology. Ergonomic criteria relevant for ASD participants not yet explored in the literature will also be investigated.**

Keywords-autism; augmented reality; museum; inclusive culture; ergonomic.

I. Introduction

This first section will give an overview of the existing litterature relative to our work about Autism Spectrum Disorders, stakes of cultural inclusion and Augmented Reality Challenges.

A. Particularities of ASD and care

France has approximately 700,000 people with Autism Spectrum Disorders (ASD), including 100,000 children. As described in the Fifth Edition of Diagnostic Manual of Mental Disorders (DSM-5) and the Eleventh Edition of International Classification of Diseases (ICD-11), social interaction and communication deficits are key characteristics of autism. People with autism are a very heterogeneous group and it is difficult to list defining symptoms. Rapid progress in technology, especially in the area of robotics, offers tremendous possibilities for innovation in treatment for individuals with Autism Spectrum Disorders (ASD). Advances in recent years have enabled robots to fulfill a variety of human-like functions, as well as to aid with the goal of improving social skills of individuals with ASD. Autistic children typically have difficulties with social interactions and cooperation. So, they might be uncooperative because they have not learned the appropriate behaviour for different social situations. Or they might not be able to manage the strong or difficult emotions, like anger, frustration or anxiety.

B. Stakes of cultural inclusion

Museums are places of culture and knowledge open to all. Unfortunately, without sufficient adaptations, many people with disabilities can find it difficult to fully enjoy these places. This project proposes the discovery and inclusion of children, teenagers and adults with disabilities in artistic culture, through augmented reality. Our desire to promote inclusive culture is fully in line with the work of the Culture-Handicap national commission set up in 2001, which is working to adapt cultural environments, particularly through digital tools. As a result, the commission has highlighted the effectiveness of augmented reality, particularly for the deaf and hard-of-hearing (Ministry of Culture, 2021). It thus affirms the need to include people with disabilities in the world of culture. However, access to culture can present challenges for people with disabilities. It is therefore necessary to adapt the activities and media on offer to enable them to access, produce and understand cultural works. Digital tools are becoming increasingly popular, and meet the adaptation needs of autistic people. There are many advantages to adapting a museum exhibition for people with disabilities. It ensures that culture is accessible to all, including people with disabilities. Indeed, disability is a social reality that affects around 20% of the French population. In addition, the use of digital tools is becoming increasingly popular, and meets the needs of autistic people in particular.

C. Augmented reality challenges

Augmented Reality (AR) is defined as a covering of our real environment with digital and computer-generated objects. They consider it to be a conceptually and historically derivative of virtual reality where users are immersed in a virtual and computer-generated environment [1]. Unlike Virtual Reality (VR), where users are isolated from their familiar surroundings and have the impression that the objects around are computer-generated [1], AR systems are designed to give users the impression that virtual objects are superimposed on real ones: they perceive both the physical environment around them and digital elements presented on top of it [1].

However, previous researchers point out a number of limitations to augmented reality. Indeed, most augmented reality applications are coded by professionals, with very little reuse possible of previously produced code [2]. One of our aims is to open up the development of augmented reality applications to non-programming professionals, and to facilitate it with efficient methods for creating and maintaining augmented reality applications.

Focusing now on the use of AR in a museum, the Art++ project give a first example of AR integration in such an environment. It was shown by the authors that augmented reality-based tours in museums would enhance users' learning abilities [3]. Visits using augmented reality increased the time spent concentrating on paintings [3].

To still illustrate the case of augmented reality used in museums, authors use the "The Ara as it Was" AR tool, which applies to Italy's Ara Pacis Museum, to gather data on the impact of augmented reality on the experience and satisfaction of museum visitors [4]. The results highlight average and high levels of satisfaction, confirming the effectiveness and innovation of augmented reality in museums. Other dimensions, such as the information provided by the museum, the enhancement of cultural heritage, and the educational dimension seem to be the most important criteria for users. Conversely, socialization, entertainment and a sense of escape are perceived as less important.

Litterature also mention the Archeoguide project [5], which "provided users with personalized 3D information on missing artifacts and reconstructed parts of damaged Greek temple sites" [2], and the Lifeplus project [6], which offers an innovative 3D reconstruction of ancient frescoes. Through these projects, it was highlighted that users like to listen and look, but not be active while using the guide [2]. Consequently, the guide should offer story-like entities without requiring the user to do too much [2]. In addition, users were happy to have more visual information, especially the 3D elements [2], but this raises an ethical question concerning the copyright of works. It is therefore possible to involve artists in the design of these 3D elements [2]. Other tips included the need for the tool to provide real-time localization on a map and a navigation guide [2]. The authors also mentioned that AR can be new to inexperienced users, so a simple interface is needed.

Other limitations and precautions to the use of AR in museums have been noted in the literature. First of all, there could be a lack of knowledge about the impact of augmented reality used in museum visits on engagement and interactions with art [3]: indeed, presently there is little literature data on user interaction with art-related augmented reality applications. A few other limitations, centered mainly on the use of a tablet as an augmented reality medium for the authors' Art++ project, were mentioned: notably the tirability of holding the tablet and the constraint of having to direct one's gaze towards different sources of information. It was also difficult to know where to focus one's attention due to too much information sources. These difficulties can be overcome by using another type of display device.

Finally, on the subject of precautions, [2] point out the importance of adjusting the size of visual markers added by augmented reality (as it is difficult to find the right size so that these markers do not hide the works of art or take up too much space). Care must also be taken not to alter the works of art too much with superimposed elements. On the other hand, the augmented reality museum guide should ideally run on affordable, lightweight, easy-to-use and robust equipment. As for the museum guide, it should not distract users' attention, so that they can observe the works of art directly as much as possible.

D. Interests of an inclusive conception

Numerous studies [7] [8] show that the use of augmented reality can increase motivation, attention and concentration and other areas affected by ASD. AR enables interaction with the real world, making it easier to discover and understand real-life situations through digital content. Other studies highlight the contribution of augmented reality with autistic children in developing fine motor skills [9] and visual attention [10] [11]. What is more, AR can be easily adapted. It thus takes advantage of the marked attraction for visual stimuli by users with ASD. This makes it possible to use this sensory modality to convey relevant information for their benefit. It thus proves to be an effective teaching aid [12].

Some authors added elements of usability applied to autism, stating that the immersion offered by augmented reality increases user engagement and motivation, which is crucial for individuals with ASD who may have attention or sensory deficits that impact their desire to learn [13]. It is also worth noting the importance of habituation, as a headset habituation program has been shown to reduce the stress caused by wearing an augmented-reality headset.

Researchers attempted to explore the potential of new technologies, and more specifically augmented reality technologies in museum settings for people with ASD [14]. To this end, they developed a support based on these technologies to make a museum visit more accessible for people with autism. The results that emerged from the experiments linked to this visit showed that augmented reality enabled significant benefits and improvements in terms of autonomy and the ability to explore the museum for people with disorders or more specifically an autism spectrum disorder.

As for the authors of [15], they gave some examples of conduct and adaptations that may be necessary when using a virtual/augmented reality headset by an ASD audience in a museum. These include site-specific features (sufficient size, calls to interact, 360° angle view of works, special effects used sparingly, works easy to handle, plurality of media types, simplicity of language), content-related elements (easy-to-read information, high contrast, large font, system for reading written text, pictograms, colorful illustrations), as well as items relating to the use of the helmet (customization of brightness, several types of support possible, several types of locomotion mode, limiting the use of fine motor skills, customization of the environment, avoiding triggers for side effects of the headset).

In short, there are few references in the literature on the use of augmented reality in cultural environments for people with ASD. However, there are already a few clues as to how to develop an augmented reality tool for such a population. The rest of the paper is structured as follows. In Section II, we present the objective of the study alongside with our main and secondary hypotheses. Then, in Section III, we describe the material and methods of the study : it emphasises participants, protocol, tools and equipment used. Section IV is dedicated to discussion and we finally conclude and discuss future work directions in Section V.

II. Hypotheses

Now, objectives and main hypotheses will be introduced.

A. Objective of the study

This project will first study the degree of acceptability of augmented reality headsets by a public of children with ASD according to pre-established criteria. It will then focus on the ergonomic evaluation of an augmented reality application used by the very same population to enhance two visit itineraries of the *Musée de L'Ecole de Nancy*, making them comprehensible and adapted to the particularities of ASD children.

B. Main hypothesis

The research problem is as follows: To what extent can augmented reality be implemented in a museum exhibition to enhance comprehension for individuals with ASD?

C. Secondary hypotheses

- Sub-hypothesis 1: When the hardware, software and content presentation criteria scores are high, subject will perceive the application as being more recreational.
- Sub-hypothesis 2: When the hardware, software and content presentation criteria scores are high, subject will perceive the application as being more educational.
- Sub-hypothesis 3: For an ASD participant, completing an AR course results in a higher educational nature perception than during a conventional course.
- Sub-hypothesis 4: For a participant with ASD, an AR tour enables them to find their way around the museum better than during a conventional tour.

III. Material and Methods

Methods will be described here through participants, the global protocol, the tools, and the equipment used.

A. Participants

Regarding the participants, it is envisaged to recruit 30 children and adolescents with autism spectrum disorder and intellectual disabilities from the various establishments of the J.B. Thiéry association in Maxeville, France. These participants are aged between 8 and 16. Ten adults participants, also with an autistic spectrum disorder and aged between 18 and 35, will be recruited from the *GEM Autisme (Groupement d'Entraide Mutuelle Autisme)* in Nancy, France.

Non-inclusion criteria for the recruitment of our participants have been implemented. We have therefore decided not to include participants with autism comorbidities, such as the presence of another neurodevelopmental disorder, participants who are prone to epilepsy or who experience headaches when wearing the augmented reality headset.

B. Protocol

The first step of the research is the development of an augmented reality application that will be used during visits to the *Musée de l'Ecole de Nancy*. This application will be divided in two parts. One will be devoted to a themed floral tour, while the other will focus on a tour about the fauna. Once participants have been recruited according to the criteria set out above, an initial test of the application will be carried out with teachers and accompanying adults. In this way, adjustments may be made in anticipation of the experimentation with participants. Then, the benefits of using augmented reality in the context of a museum visit for an ASD public will be assessed during the experimental phase.

C. Tools

Now, the evaluation tools expected to be used in the research will be introduced. Some of these have been found in the literature, while others have been designed specifically for the study.

1) Ergonomic evaluation grid: The first tool that has been developed, which is also the focus of our experimentation, concerns the ergonomic evaluation of the augmented reality headset. After reviewing the literature, there was so far no exhaustive ergonomic evaluation grid established for such a device. In fact, only a few papers focusing on AR mentioned some of the relevant ergonomic criteria that should be assessed without drafting a holistic list. The grid lists the criteria already present in the literature alongside with added elements that are relevant to the object of study (augmented reality applied to a museum context) and to ASD participants (Table 1).

The grid is broken down into several dimensions: criteria relating to the hardware, the software, the behaviour of the participants, the presentation of the content of the application and visit as well as criteria relating to the secondary effects caused by wearing the headset and the cognitive cost of completing the visit.

The hardware ergonomic criteria focus on a number of important points relating to the headset use. For each participant, the perceived weight of the headset, temperature, tactile acceptance, battery life, balance of the back of the helmet, intuitive handling, adjustability, overall comfort, noise level and ease of use will be assessed. All this information will whether the equipment used is suitable for ASD participants or not.

Criteria relating to the software aspect will focus on the accessibility of the controls, hand tracking by the augmented reality headset, the fluidity of eye tracking, the degree of adaptation and the options offered to the user, the legibility of the route, the content of the activities and the relevance of the information presented. The educational and entertaining nature of the augmented reality application will also be evaluated. The assessment of these ergonomic criteria will bring out relevant modifications and adjustments to implement to the application in a user-centered approach.

The user's behaviour during the visit will also be observed. Notes will be taken about the user's mood, the interactions they initiate, their exploration of the space with their eyes and their ability to find their way around the space. This will bring out an overall view of the effects of the device on the participants conduct.

About the presentation of the content, care will be taken to ensure the simplicity of the interface and menus, the legibility and clarity of the images and the appropriate size of the text and images. Those pieces of information will be invaluable in assessing the accessibility of our application.

Finally, attention will be paid to any side effects associated with the use of the headset (such as nausea, dizziness, loss of balance, visual fatigue, headaches, etc.). The cognitive cost of completing the course will also be quantified using tests that will be presented further. Due to the potential tiredness of ASD people, it will be relevant to have an overview of the cognitive load induced by visiting the museum with the augmented reality device.

Most of these criteria will be assessed on the basis of observation and interviews. However, some of them will require the use of additional tools or the conduct of activities. In that way, to assess the educational nature of the application, it may be necessary to ask the participants to draw up a narrative diagram of the activities carried out, to put in order images in order to reconstruct the visit, to associate the images with the museum rooms visited or to take the reverse route of the visit and explain what has been seen. In the same way, the cognitive cost of the tour will be observed on the basis of psychometric tests: the comparison between the performance of short-term memory / inhibition at the beginning and at the end of the tour seems to be a good indicator of that cognitive load.

2) Inhibition assessment: To assess the cognitive cost induced by completing the augmented reality course, it is planned to evaluate inhibition performance. With this in mind,

TABLE I. ERGONOMIC ASSESSMENT GRID.

Hardware	
1. Weight	1: External battery plugged in
	2: Without external battery
2. Temperature	
3. Tactile acceptance	
4. Battery life	
5. Balance of the headset	1: With the base strap
	2: With the rear support
6. Intuitive handling	
7. Adjustability	
8. Overall comfort	
9. Noise level	1: With the fan plugged in
	2: Without the fan
10. Ease of use	
11. Portability	
Software	
12. Accessibility of controls	
13. Headset hands tracking	
14. Fluidity of eye tracking	
15. Degree of adaptation/options proposed to the user	1: For the headset OS
	2: For the application
16. Clarity of the route	1: Through the museum
	2: About points of interest
17. Activities	
18. Playfulness perceived by the user	
19. Educational nature of the application	
20. Relevance of the presented information	1: Audio information
	2: Visual information
Behaviour	
21. Thymia	1: Overall thymia
	2: Frustration
	3: Evolution of the mood
22. Interactions induced by the use of the headset	
23. Exploring space with the eyes	
24. Situate oneself in space	
Presentation	
25. Simplicity of interface and menus	
26. Image legibility and sharpness	1: At arm's length
	2: At a distance of 4 meters
27. Size of text and images	
Others	
28. Presence of side effects during use	
29. Cognitive cost of the visit	1: Short-term memory
	2: Inhibition

a Stroop effect test has been extracted from the literature which is based on a theme corresponding to one of the two thematic courses of the application (the wildlife theme). It allows us to rediscover the Stroop effect with boards based on animals known to the general public [16]. Its principle is to inhibit the quasi-automatic reading of an animal word-name in order to name the animal presented in an associated image.

The Stroop effect is preserved despite the change in medium type for the following reasons: The test offers a control board where the written word corresponds to the image of the animal, so the interference phenomenon does not occur. In addition, the second board displays a word that does not match the subsequent image (Figure 1). Finally, the words and images refer to animals that are well known to everyone. As a result, there is no risk of semantic complexity interfering with the smooth running of the test (as well as in the classic Stroop test with colours).

To be as faithful and close as possible to the original Stroop effect test, it is planned to run the control condition before the interfering condition.

Still to assess inhibition, but this time for the second course on the theme of flora, it is envisaged to adapt the Stroop effect

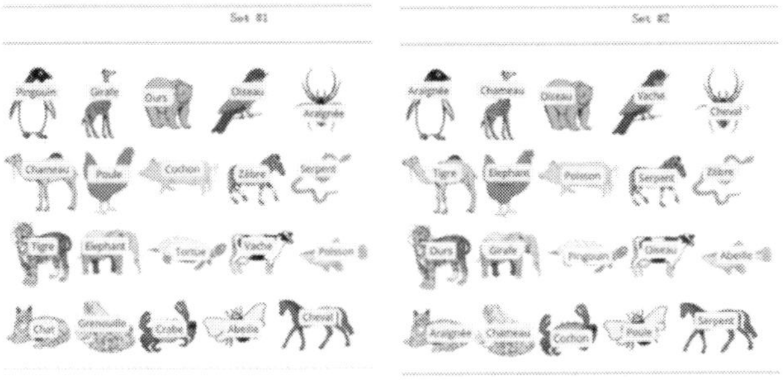

Figure 1. Stroop Effect Test based on animals [16].

that has just been presented [16] to the theme of the plants.

Based on the authors mode of presentation, the animal theme will be transposed to a plant theme by replacing the images and names of animals with fruits and vegetables: these will be familiar to the general public, easily recognizable and will not present any phonological complexity (fewer than 3 syllables) in order to preserve the purity of the test. The Stroop effect is preserved despite the change in the type of support because of the following reasons: The test proposes a control condition in which the written word corresponds to the image of the fruit or vegetable and therefore the interference phenomenon does not occur. In addition of that, the second condition displays a word that does not match the subsequent image: an interference occurs when the word is read before the plant is named (Figure 2). Finally, the words and images referring to fruits and vegetables are well known to everyone. As a result, there is no risk of semantic complexity interfering with the test (as in the original Stroop effect test with colours).

In order to be faithful and as close as possible to the original test, the control condition will be passed before the interfering condition. Furthermore, to be close to the material of [16], images with a similar graphic style will be used for our plates.

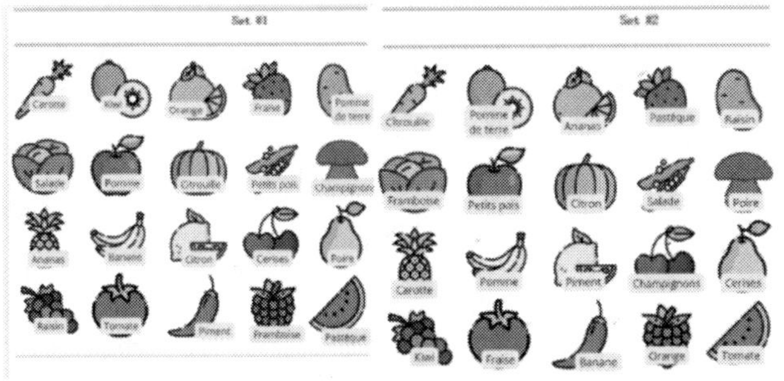

Figure 2. Stroop Effect Test based on plants (adapted from [16]).

3) Short-term memory: To complete the assessment of the cognitive cost of visiting the museum, a second dimension will be evaluated, namely short-term memory. To this end, a short-term memory test has been extracted from the literature called 'Animal Race' which is perfectly suited for the wildlife trail part of the application. Thereafter, this test has been adapted to the theme of flora for the second plant-based route.

For the first route (wildlife route), the participant is asked to name the order of arrival of animals in a race after the examiner has verbally given the order of arrival. The number of animals involved in the race varied from 2 to 7, enabling memory span to be measured.

The animal race test has been chosen because it has the advantage of not involving language to any great extent, and is therefore accessible to as many people as possible. That choice has also been made because of this test ability to isolate working memory. There are a number of reasons for this: first, the animals have short and simple names that do not require overly complex phonological processing. In addition, the animals used in the test are familiar to everyone and it is easy to associate them with images: there will therefore be no interference from semantic complexity during the assessment.

As for the flora trail, the animal race test has been adapted to a plant-based version. The subject will be asked to rank plants according to their development and highest growth.

Based on the reference article on the animal race, four criteria emerge for choosing the plants to be ranked: Firstly, the plants should have a short, simple name that does not require overly complex phonological processing (to avoid any form of phonologically induced overload). Ideally, they should be monosyllabic. Next, the word associated with the plant should be familiar to everyone as far as possible, and its semantic association easy. This is to avoid any bias due to the potentially complex meaning of the words. In addition, the plants must be linked to pictograms that are easily recognizable and presented in a common graphic style. Finally, 7 different plants had to be implemented in order to cover a memory span of 7 items as in the original test.

In addition to that, to respect the race principle, the plant presented first by the examiner will have the highest growth and so on in descending order. Also, each item in the plant race will be associated with an item in the baseline test, in a such way that the word presentation order will be identical to the original test.

Figure 3. Pictograms used for our adaptation of the animal race test entitled 'the plant race'.

D. Equipment

Regarding the equipment, it is planned to use Meta Quest 3 headsets of the Meta brand. To ensure a better balance between the front and back of the headset, an additional strap will be clipped to the device.

IV. Discussion

The use of Augmented Reality (AR) in museums is an emerging field that holds significant potential, especially for enhancing accessibility among populations with specific needs, such as individuals with Autism Spectrum Disorders (ASD).

Figure 4. Meta Quest 3 picture.

Most existing studies have utilized tablet-based AR technologies, which, despite their documented advantages, present certain ergonomic drawbacks. Tablets can induce user fatigue due to prolonged carrying and create divided attention between the screen and physical exhibits. In contrast, AR headsets have the potential to mitigate these limitations, offering a more immersive, hands-free experience that allows users to engage directly with artworks without the distraction of constantly shifting their gaze.

In exploring the implementation of AR headsets within museums, particular attention must be given to the ergonomic and ethical considerations. Ergonomic criteria, such as device weight, ease of handling, comfort, visual clarity, and adaptability to individual user needs, are crucial to ensure effective and comfortable usage, particularly for users with ASD, who may exhibit heightened sensory sensitivities or distinct interaction patterns. The evaluation grid developed in this study specifically targets these ergonomic criteria, providing comprehensive insights into the suitability of AR headsets for this audience.

From a methodological perspective, the current project addresses a notable gap by systematically comparing AR-guided museum tours using headsets with traditional museum visits. This approach allows for rigorous evaluation of AR's actual impact on visitor engagement, comprehension, and overall experience.

V. Conclusion and Future Work

This Work in Progress article gives us the opportunity to present our theoretical foundations. This was followed by a description of our methodology and the results we hoped to achieve. Finally, the discussion highlighted the implications that this research could have on the scientific landscape.

New evaluation tools developed specifically for this research, including ergonomic assessment grids, cognitive load evaluations through psychometric tests, and observational methods, provide robust mechanisms to measure not only usability but also educational and recreational outcomes. The evaluation of the relevance of these tools will be a part of our future work.

Ultimately, this project will deliver valuable empirical insights into the advantages and limitations of AR headset use within museum settings for individuals with ASD, highlighting critical ergonomic factors and the necessity of personalization. The results will contribute significantly to inclusive cultural practices. This will allow us to developp in the future practical guidelines for subsequent developments in accessible AR museum technologies.

References

[1] E. Costanza, A. Kunz, and M. Fjeld, "Mixed Reality: A Survey," in *Human Machine Interaction*, D. Lalanne and J. Kohlas, Eds., vol. 5440, Series Title: Lecture Notes in Computer Science, Berlin, Heidelberg: Springer Berlin Heidelberg, 2009, pp. 47–68, ISBN: 978-3-642-00436-0 978-3-642-00437-7. DOI: 10.1007/978-3-642-00437-7_3.

[2] D. Abawi *et al.*, *A Mixed Reality Museum Guide : The challenges and its realization*, 2004.

[3] T. Aitamurto, J.-B. Boin, K. Chen, A. Cherif, and S. Shridhar, "The Impact of Augmented Reality on Art Engagement: Liking, Impression of Learning, and Distraction," en, in *Virtual, Augmented and Mixed Reality: Applications in Health, Cultural Heritage, and Industry*, J. Y. Chen and G. Fragomeni, Eds., vol. 10910, Series Title: Lecture Notes in Computer Science, Cham: Springer International Publishing, 2018, pp. 153–171, ISBN: 978-3-319-91583-8 978-3-319-91584-5. DOI: 10.1007/978-3-319-91584-5_13.

[4] M. Trunfio and S. Campana, "A visitors' experience model for mixed reality in the museum," en, *Current Issues in Tourism*, vol. 23, no. 9, pp. 1053–1058, May 2020, ISSN: 1368-3500, 1747-7603. DOI: 10.1080/13683500.2019.1586847.

[5] *The ARCHEOGUIDE (Augmented Reality-based Cultural Heritage On-Site Guide – IST-1999-11306) Project Homepage*, 2004.

[6] *The Lifeplus*, 2004.

[7] A. Dechsling *et al.*, "Virtual and Augmented Reality in Social Skills Interventions for Individuals with Autism Spectrum Disorder: A Scoping Review," en, *Journal of Autism and Developmental Disorders*, vol. 52, no. 11, pp. 4692–4707, Nov. 2022, ISSN: 0162-3257, 1573-3432. DOI: 10 . 1007 / s10803-021-05338-5.

[8] M. Wedyan *et al.*, "Augmented Reality for Autistic Children to Enhance Their Understanding of Facial Expressions," en, *Multimodal Technologies and Interaction*, vol. 5, no. 8, p. 48, Aug. 2021, ISSN: 2414-4088. DOI: 10.3390/mti5080048.

[9] M. Magrini *et al.*, "Augmented Interaction Systems for Supporting Autistic Children. Evolution of a Multichannel Expressive Tool: The SEMI Project Feasibility Study," en, *Applied Sciences*, vol. 9, no. 15, p. 3081, Jul. 2019, ISSN: 2076-3417. DOI: 10.3390/app9153081.

[10] C. H. Chen, C.-H. Ho, and J.-B. Lin, "The Development of an Augmented Reality Game-based Learning Environment," en, *Procedia - Social and Behavioral Sciences*, vol. 174, pp. 216–220, Feb. 2015, ISSN: 18770428. DOI: 10.1016/j.sbspro.2015.01.649.

[11] C. Papoutsi, A. Drigas, and C. Skianis, "Virtual and Augmented Reality for Developing Emotional Intelligence Skills," *International Journal of Recent Contributions from Engineering, Science & IT (iJES)*, vol. 9, no. 3, p. 35, Sep. 2021, ISSN: 2197-8581. DOI: 10.3991/ijes.v9i3.23939.

[12] D. F. Cihak *et al.*, "Evaluating Augmented Reality to Complete a Chain Task for Elementary Students With Autism," en, *Journal of Special Education Technology*, vol. 31, no. 2, pp. 99–108, Jun. 2016, ISSN: 0162-6434, 2381-3121. DOI: 10.1177/0162643416651724.

[13] M. Leharanger, E. A. Rodriguez Martinez, O. Balédent, and L. Vandromme, "Familiarization with Mixed Reality for Individuals with Autism Spectrum Disorder: An Eye Tracking Study," en, *Sensors*, vol. 23, no. 14, p. 6304, Jul. 2023, ISSN: 1424-8220. DOI: 10.3390/s23146304.

[14] C. Giaconi, A. Ascenzi, N. Del Bianco, I. D'angelo, and S. A. Capellini, "Virtual and Augmented Reality for the Cultural Accessibility of People with Autism Spectrum Disorders: A Pilot Study," *The International Journal of the Inclusive Museum*, vol. 14, no. 1, pp. 95–106, 2021, ISSN: 1835-2014, 1835-2022. DOI: 10.18848/1835-2014/CGP/v14i01/95-106.

[15] A. Caldarelli *et al.*, "Co-designing Immersive and Inclusive Virtual Museum with children and People with Disabilities: A Pilot Study," in *2022 International Conference on Computational Science and Computational Intelligence (CSCI)*, Las Vegas, NV, USA: IEEE, Dec. 2022, pp. 1964–1969, ISBN: 979-8-3503-2028-2. DOI: 10.1109/CSCI58124.2022.00353.

[16] K. De Bot and F. Fang, "Circadian rhythms and second language performance," *Studies in Second Language Learning and Teaching*, vol. 7, no. 1, pp. 47–60, Mar. 2017, ISSN: 2084-1965, 2083-5205. DOI: 10.14746/ssllt.2017.7.1.3.

The Effects of Virtualization on Connectedness, Presence, and Immersion: A Mixed-Methods Comparison of Real, Mixed, and Virtual Environments

Niklas Groffner
Faculty of Computer Science and Business Information Systems
University of Applied Sciences Würzburg-Schweinfurt
Würzburg, Germany
e-mail: niklas.groffner@study.thws.de

Abstract— **Virtual environments are increasingly integrated into diverse domains, redefining how individuals perceive and interact with their surroundings. These environments hold significant potential to influence human experiences, particularly through the dimensions of presence, connectedness, and immersion. Understanding these concepts is essential for optimizing the design and application of virtual systems in education, healthcare, and other societal contexts. This research examines the impact of virtualization on the perception of presence, connectedness, and immersion by comparing real-world, mixed, and fully virtual environments using a mixed-methods approach. The qualitative analysis engaged 5 participants exploring object interactions across real, MR, and VR settings, while the quantitative analysis, involving 31 participants, assessed introductory games specifically in MR and VR scenarios. Results indicate that connectedness is strongest in real-world scenarios, diminishing with increased virtualization, while immersion and presence show no significant variance across environments. The lack of physical feedback and reduced sensory stimuli in VR and MR environments were primary contributors to these differences. The findings underscore the necessity of real interactions in education and healthcare, suggesting consumer protection measures for Virtual and Mixed Reality environments.**

Keywords— ***Extended Reality; Presence; Immersion; Connectedness.***

I. INTRODUCTION

Mixed Reality (MR) and Virtual Reality (VR) create new realities that deeply impact our experiences. For instance, VR enables immersive training simulations for medical personnel [1] and revolutionizes customer experiences in retail [2]. In the entertainment industry, VR introduces new forms of cinema and interactive experiences [3]. MR is used to create realistic educational environments that enhance learners' presence and engagement [4]. This raises the question of how these technologies influence fundamental aspects of our reality.

This study examines the key concepts of presence, immersion, and connectedness in the context of VR and MR to understand how different levels of virtualization affect our perception and interactions. The significance of this research lies in gaining a deeper understanding of how these technologies shape human experience and behavior. The impact on the perception of presence, immersion, and connectedness is particularly important, as these factors significantly alter user experience in VR and MR applications, as this study demonstrates.

Despite numerous studies analyzing individual aspects of VR and MR [5][6], comprehensive investigations comparing these technologies with each other and with the real world are lacking. This study addresses this research gap by comparatively examining how experienced connectedness, presence, and immersion differ in VR, MR, and real environments.

The primary aim of this research is to systematically explore the impact of Extended Reality (XR) on experiential factors such as connectedness, presence, and immersion using a mixed-methods framework. This objective is subdivided into two specific goals: (1) The qualitative goal focuses on exploring participant perceptions of XR in terms of presence, immersion, and connectedness, aiming to extract deep insights into subjective experiences across diverse environments. Key themes and patterns discerned from this analysis inform the hypothesis development. This qualitative analysis identifies central themes and patterns that serve as the basis for hypothesis formation. (2) The quantitative goal investigates whether varying levels of environmental virtualization significantly affect participants' perceived connectedness to themselves, others, and the broader world. The qualitative analysis suggests that the perception of connectedness may be influenced by the degree of virtualization. These indications are tested in the quantitative analysis, with particular attention to the dimensions of connectedness.

These objectives lead to specific research questions. The qualitative research questions are: How is XR perceived in terms of presence, immersion, and connectedness by the participants? What central themes and patterns can be identified from the subjective experiences and perceptions of participants in various Virtual Environments (VE)? The quantitative research question is: Does the degree of virtualization of an environment significantly influence the perception of experienced connectedness? These questions guide the qualitative and quantitative investigation to gain a comprehensive understanding of the impact of XR on the experience of connectedness, presence, and immersion.

The study is divided into six sections to ensure a clear and comprehensible structure. In Section 1, the study introduces the topic and outlines the objectives of the study, explaining the specific research questions and the methodology used to address them. Section 2 lays the theoretical foundation, focusing on the concepts of connectedness, presence, and immersion. Section 3 describes the methodological approach, explaining the use of a mixed-methods methodology that includes both qualitative and quantitative approaches. It details the selection of methods, data collection, and analysis to ensure the research's transparency and validity. Section 4 presents the study's results, starting with the qualitative analysis followed by the quantitative analysis. It includes descriptive statistics and inferential statistical tests conducted to verify the hypotheses. Section 5 discusses the results in the context of existing scientific literature, explaining the implications for theory and practice. It critically reflects on the study's methodological weaknesses, highlighting potential limitations. In Section 6, the study summarizes the key findings, emphasizes the relevance of the results for the development of XR technologies, and outlines future research directions. It demonstrates how VR and MR influence the sense of connectedness, presence, and immersion, and outlines practical applications.

II. Theoretical Foundations

A. *Definition and theoretical construct of connectedness*

This study explores the concept of connectedness based on the theoretical framework proposed by Watts et al. [7]. According to Watts et al. [7], connectedness is defined as a state of feeling connected to oneself, others, and the world. The dimension of self-connectedness is often experienced in therapeutic contexts and involves a deep sense of connection with one's senses, body, and emotions [7]. It arises through awareness, acceptance, and alignment of one's behavior with this awareness [8]. Social connectedness refers to the feeling of belonging and attachment to other people and communities [9]. Watts et al. [7] describe this as the view of oneself in relation to others, cognitive structures of interpersonal relationships, and the perception of isolation. Social relationships significantly contribute to physical and mental health and act as a protective factor against depression [7]. Connectedness with others is fostered through empathy and sharing emotional experiences [10]. Connectedness to the world is described as transpersonal experiences and a sense of connection to nature and a larger spiritual principle [7]. This dimension includes an expanded self-awareness that encompasses the individual's relationship with the world and the universe [7]. Phillips-Salimi et al. [11] also describe connectedness as a multidimensional concept involving emotional closeness to others, a sense of community and belonging, and engagement in social networks. Essential characteristics of these social relationships include intimacy, empathy, trust, and reciprocity [11].

B. *Definition and theoretical construct of presence*

Slater and Wilbur [12] describe presence as a multifaceted concept that conveys the subjective feeling of actually being in a specific environment, whether real or virtual. This state of consciousness can be related to immersion and the sensation of being in a particular setting. Presence affects aspects of autonomous responses and behavior in a VE [12].

According to Witmer and Singer [13], the feeling of presence in VEs depends on various factors, including the quality of sensory impressions and the technology's ability to mask physical reality. Presence is described as the subjective experience of truly being in an environment, even if the body is physically elsewhere. The authors believe that presence is a normal consciousness phenomenon requiring focused attention and is based on the interaction between sensory stimuli, environmental factors that promote engagement and immersion, and internal tendencies towards involvement [13]. The feeling of presence is often enhanced by immersion, which describes the technological properties that enable immersion in the virtual world [12].

Presence, as described by Slater and Wilbur [12] in their work A Framework for Immersive Virtual Environments (FIVE), is a central theoretical model in this analysis. This model is used as a theoretical construct to examine the subjective experience of presence in VEs. It provides a comprehensive framework for investigating the design of VEs. Slater and Wilbur [12] state that participants who experience a high level of presence should perceive the VE as a more engaging reality than the surrounding physical world. This intense feeling leads to the environment created by the displays being perceived as real places rather than mere seen images. Another important aspect of presence is the ability to remove the participant from everyday reality and place them in an alternative, self-contained world with its own actions and dynamics. This dimension of presence, which Slater and Wilbur call "plot," allows participants to act and interact in the VE, further enhancing the feeling of presence [12].

Slater [14] introduced Place Illusion (PI) and Plausibility Illusion (Psi), distinguishing between the sensation of being in a virtual space and the credibility of the scenario [14]. Later, Slater et al. [15] emphasized that both PI and Psi are essential for realistic user responses in virtual environments [15].

C. *Definition and theoretical construct of immersion*

Immersion is a central concept in the field of VEs. This thesis primarily utilizes the theoretical framework of Witmer and Singer to examine immersion. Witmer and Singer [13] define immersion as a psychological state where an individual perceives being surrounded by an environment, continuously receiving stimuli and experiences. Factors influencing immersion include isolation from the physical environment, perception of involvement in the VE, natural interaction and control capabilities, and the perception of self-movement within the VE. The use of head-mounted displays is crucial as they obscure the physical environment and create a sense of isolation. Additionally, natural interaction enhances immersion; when users can interact and control the VE naturally, their immersion is strengthened. The perception of self-movement, or the feeling of navigating within the VE, is also a key aspect of immersion [13].

Slater [16] offers another theoretical construct for explaining immersion. He defines immersion as the ability of a VR system to simulate a realistic VE. The better the system mimics reality, the higher the degree of immersion. A system that involves the entire body in perception offers higher immersion than one that only allows viewing a screen. A system's capacity to replicate another is recognized as a fundamental metric for assessing immersion. A highly immersive system could simulate the experience of a less immersive one. Researchers can use these differences to study how the illusion of being in the virtual world and people's reactions to events in the virtual world are influenced by the degree of immersion [16].

Immersion is not merely a property of the system or technology enabling the experience. It is a state of deep mental engagement where awareness of the physical environment is reduced or completely dissociated due to a shift in attention [17].

Nilsson et al. [18] conduct a comprehensive analysis and categorize existing definitions of immersion into three categories: as a system property, as a subjective response to narrative content, or as a subjective response to challenges in VEs. This three-dimensional taxonomy is used to discuss how different theories of presence relate to various definitions of immersion [18].

D. *Synergy of Connectedness, Immersion, and Presence*

The study of connectedness, immersion, and presence is essential for a comprehensive understanding of user experience in various forms of reality, such as reality, MR and VR. These three aspects are closely interlinked and mutually reinforcing, enabling a profound analysis of the emotional and cognitive effects elicited by these different environments.

To further explore the complex relationships between these aspects, it is helpful to examine the role of immersion as a central component in VEs. Smith and Mulligan [19] note that various manipulations of immersion, such as field of view, audiovisual effects, and light realism, can have different impacts on memory and presence. Studies indicate that immersion in VR environments not only affects presence but also other factors like interactivity and user satisfaction. These findings are supported by Mütterlein [20], who investigates the interactions between immersion, presence, and interactivity in a VR context. Her study shows that both presence and interactivity significantly contribute to immersion, with interactivity further enhancing presence. Immersion proves to be an important predictor of user satisfaction in VEs [20]. Additionally, Servotte et al. [1] find that the feeling of presence in VR correlates with individual tendencies towards immersion. Advanced students with a higher tendency towards immersion report a stronger sense of presence. Despite an increase in stress levels during immersion, the sense of presence remains high and the level of cybersickness low [1]. These findings highlight that not only the technical design of the VR environment but also individual user differences play a crucial role in the emergence of presence and immersion.

Various factors can affect both the sense of presence and connectedness in VEs. McCreery et al. [21] find that continuous character development and socialization make the connectedness between the participant and their avatar so strong that it ultimately becomes more important for the sense of presence than media and environmental properties. A study by Young et al. [22] shows that VR can foster emotional connectedness through immersive experiences. By adopting the perspective of a protagonist in the first person and empathizing with their experiences through visual, auditory, and haptic elements, deep immersion is achieved. This intense immersion allows users to form a strong emotional bond with the protagonist, as they not only see and hear but also feel what the protagonist experiences [22].

E. *Survey Instruments*

For this study, specific questionnaires are selected and modified to collect both qualitative and quantitative data. The questionnaires used include the Watts Connectedness Scale (WCS) [23] for assessing connectedness, the Slater-Usoh-Steed (SUS) questionnaire [24] for measuring the sense of presence and the questionnaire by Tcha-Tokey et al. [25] for measuring immersion.

The WCS, developed by Watts et al. [7][23], measures three key dimensions of connectedness: connectedness to oneself, to others, and to the world. The scale assesses how strongly a person feels connected to their own senses, body, and emotions, as well as emotional closeness and a sense of community with others. Additionally, the WCS measures the feeling of belonging to nature and the global context, including spiritual and transpersonal connections [7][23]. A significant advantage of the WCS is that it captures multiple dimensions of connectedness simultaneously, allowing for a nuanced analysis of social experiences. This comprehensive approach ensures that all relevant dimensions of social and personal connectedness are considered, enabling a deeper and more differentiated analysis of participants' social experiences. The WCS is based on the theoretical foundations of Watts et al. [7]. The validity of the WCS questionnaire is confirmed through extensive testing, showing high correlations between the WCS scales and other related scales measuring psychological flexibility, well-being, social connectedness, nature connectedness, and anxiety [7]. These high correlations demonstrate the convergent validity of the WCS, indicating that the questionnaire reliably captures the various dimensions of connectedness.

The SUS questionnaire [24] is a recognized instrument for measuring the sense of presence in VEs and is used in various studies as a useful tool for differentiating experiences in real and virtual contexts. The questionnaire captures three key dimensions: the feeling of actually being in the VE, the extent to which the VE becomes the primary reality, and the memory of the VE as a real place. These measurements are closely related to the theoretical framework of the FIVE model by Slater and Wilbur, which is used to study presence [24].

The questionnaire developed by Tcha-Tokey et al. [25] covers several key aspects of user experience, including presence, engagement, immersion, flow, usability, skill, emotion, experience consequence, judgment, and technology adoption [25]. However, for this study, only the section on immersion is selected, as it is concise and focused, precisely measuring the depth of participants' immersion experiences. The immersion section of the Tcha-Tokey et al. [25] questionnaire is based on the Immersion Tendency Questionnaire by Witmer and Singer [13], which forms the theoretical basis of this study's construct. The validation of the questionnaire shows reliability and sensitivity, even for the immersion section [25]. The specifically selected immersion section provides comprehensive insights into participants' immersion experiences despite its brevity, making it suitable for this study.

III. METHODOLOGY

A. Mixed-Methods Approach

For this study, selected questionnaires were used in both confirmatory quantitative and exploratory qualitative analyses. Modifications allowed for detailed qualitative insights into participants' subjective experiences, enhancing data analysis depth. Validated questionnaires increased reliability and validity. Hypotheses examined the impact of virtualization on perceived connectedness. Qualitative interviews provided insights into experiences in reality, MR, and VR, leading to two opposing hypotheses. These were tested and statistically evaluated using quantitative methods. Pilot testing validated and optimized questions, scenarios, and data collection methods. To ensure the generalizability of results, no restrictions were placed on demographic variables, allowing for a diverse participant sample. Real-world experiences serve as a benchmark for evaluating immersion, presence, and connectedness in virtual and mixed settings.

B. Qualitative Methodology

The qualitative methodology of this study explored how presence, immersion, and connectedness are experienced in real, MR, and VR environments. An experimental approach was used, ensuring maximum possible comparability across settings. Although the tasks do not cover the entire spectrum of XR applications, they were carefully selected to reflect realistic use cases, enhancing ecological validity where possible. Each participant completed tasks in all three realities—utilizing real objects in the real environment, a combination of real and virtual elements in MR, and solely virtual elements in VR. In the object-finding task, participants located and placed tennis balls using real, mixed, or virtual elements depending on the environment. For the painting task, they engaged with either real artworks or virtual representations to assess emotional responses and presence. The plant-watering task involved using real and virtual watering cans to tend to real or virtual plants.

Figure 1. Plant casting task in the MR (created with Figmin XR)

The MR environment used the Meta Quest 3 [26], while the VR environment used the Oculus Rift S [27]. The selection of these head-mounted displays was driven by optimization criteria for each specific application. Although different headsets were used, potential biases were minimized by selecting devices with comparable technical specifications and user experience characteristics. The VR experiment was conducted at the University of Applied Sciences Würzburg-Schweinfurt, using Unity [28] to construct an intricate representation of the physical space, alongside Sketchfab [29] models. Figmin XR [30] was used for MR tasks.

Strict ethical standards were maintained, with informed consent and anonymized data. Participants, aged 23 to 55, were selected based on VR and MR experience and technological affinity, resulting in 5 participants.

Semi-structured interviews, averaging 22 minutes per scenario, were conducted and transcribed manually. The interview guide followed Misoch's [31] recommendations, covering presence, immersion, and connectedness. Modified questionnaires were used, with closed questions converted into open-ended ones to gain more detailed insights. Presence questions were based on the SUS questionnaire [24], immersion questions on Tcha-Tokey et al. [25], and connectedness questions on the WCS [23].

Thematic coding identified patterns in participants' experiences across environments. Case summaries and descriptive analyses supported the findings.

C. Quantitative Methodology

The quantitative methodology aimed to systematically investigate perceived connectedness and the impact of virtualization. Based on qualitative insights, the null hypothesis (H_0) posited no impact of virtualization on connectedness, while the alternative hypothesis (H_1) suggested higher virtualization weakens this perception.

The quantitative component employed an experimental design, randomly assigning participants to MR or VR conditions to minimize order effects and facilitate causal inference. To ensure a comprehensive dataset, each participant engaged with all three scenarios, namely reality, MR, and VR. They completed standardized questionnaires reflecting on recent real-world experiences and then interacted with either MR or VR applications. The study was conducted in a controlled lab environment to ensure data comparability.

However, it is important to note that the scenarios were not fully comparable across environments. The applications

"First Encounter" [32] (MR) and "First Contact" [33] (VR) were chosen for their role as playful introduction games designed to familiarize users with the fundamental interactions of VR and MR using the Meta Quest 3. The selection of these applications was made because they simulate typical interactions and challenges encountered in real-world XR scenarios, thereby enhancing the ecological validity of the study and offering realistic interactions particularly relevant in the XR industry. The global VR market, estimated at $12.3 billion in 2023, is growing at a projected average annual growth rate of over 23%, with the gaming industry being a significant driver of this growth [34]. For the real-world scenario, participants were instructed: "Think of a moment when you recently discovered or explored something new." This instruction served as the real-world baseline, without the use of any specific app or task.

Strict ethical standards were maintained, with informed consent and anonymized data. Participants, aged 18 to 70, were recruited based on diverse backgrounds and technology experiences, resulting in 31 participants.

The variables examined included the degree of virtualization as the independent variable and perceived connectedness as the dependent variable, evaluated using the questionnaires outlined in the Survey Instruments Section. Immersion and presence were treated as secondary variables, also assessed using these instruments, and these measurements involved a sample of only 5 participants. Data analysis involved descriptive and inferential statistics using JASP [35]. The Shapiro-Wilk test was used to check data normality. Parametric tests (paired *t*-tests) were used for normally distributed data, while non-parametric tests (Wilcoxon signed-rank tests) were used for non-normally distributed data. A significance level of 0.05 was set.

This methodological approach facilitated valid insights into the effects of virtualization on connectedness. Statistical evaluations were conducted with significance determined at *p*-values below 0.05, and effect sizes calculated to ascertain practical relevance.

IV. Results

A. *Qualitative Results*

The results revealed nuanced differences in the subjective experiences of participants, which were critically analyzed to identify recurring patterns and deviations.

The findings pertaining to presence underscored its dependence on attention, a sense of being, and the clarity of memory. In the real environment, participants demonstrated consistently high levels of attention, with their presence marked by an acute awareness of their surroundings and vividly clear memories of the experiences. The qualitative accounts suggest that the tangibility of the real environment and the natural continuity of interactions were instrumental in sustaining this strong sense of presence. In MR, presence remained robust yet exhibited slight variability due to the duality of real and virtual elements. While many participants appreciated the added richness of MR, they also noted occasional challenges in maintaining focus or seamlessly integrating the two layers of reality. By contrast, VR posed distinct challenges to presence, as some participants reported diminished attention or felt disconnected from the immersive environment, attributing these effects to its artificial nature or technological limitations. However, others found the novelty of the VR experience engaging, which heightened their attention and focus.

Immersion, a pivotal construct in the study, was deeply influenced by individual preferences and the participants' expectations of the environments. In VR, participants who perceived the virtual environment as sufficiently high-quality and engaging reported profound immersion, characterized by deep emotional and cognitive involvement. However, for others, technological shortcomings or a perceived lack of realism detracted from their ability to fully engage with the virtual environment. MR, while offering a more balanced integration of real-world familiarity and virtual novelty, elicited diverse responses. Several participants described MR as enabling a unique, albeit somewhat partial, sense of immersion, reflecting both the strengths and inherent limitations of blending real and virtual elements. The real environment, conversely, evoked a stable yet less dynamic form of immersion, anchored in the predictability of familiar settings.

Connectedness, encompassing emotional and physical bonds with oneself, others, and the broader environment, exhibited a clear inverse relationship with the degree of virtualization. Participants consistently reported the strongest feelings of connectedness in the real environment, which they attributed to direct sensory feedback, natural social interactions, and the inherent authenticity of their surroundings. In MR, connectedness was notably weaker, as participants often struggled to reconcile the duality of real and virtual elements. VR elicited the lowest levels of connectedness, with several participants describing a pronounced sense of isolation. This phenomenon was particularly evident in their qualitative accounts, where descriptions of VR environments frequently included metaphors of detachment and enclosure, such as being "sealed in a bubble" or "cut off from the outside world." These findings suggest that the abstraction inherent in virtual environments may undermine the fundamental human need for tangible and reciprocal interactions.

To build upon these findings, hypotheses were derived to formalize the observed relationships between virtualization and its effects on connectedness. The null hypothesis (H_0) posited that the degree of virtualization exerts no influence on connectedness across its various dimensions. In contrast, the alternative hypothesis (H_1) proposed that increasing levels of virtualization, from reality to MR and VR, progressively diminish connectedness. These hypotheses, while rooted in the qualitative observations, were designed to guide subsequent quantitative analyses, thereby enabling the systematic validation of theoretical assumptions.

The transition to a quantitative approach sought to empirically test these hypotheses through standardized instruments designed to measure presence, immersion, and connectedness across the three environments.

TABLE I. *T*-TEST FOR PAIRED VARIABLES OF THE WCS

Variable 1	*Variable 2*	*t*	*p*	*Cohen's d*
WCS in reality	WCS in MR	5.798	< 0.001	1.041
WCS in reality	WCS in VR	5.321	< 0.001	0.956
WCS in MR	WCS in VR	-0.023	0.982	-0.004

B. *Quantitative Results*

The descriptive statistics indicated a clear decline in connectedness as the degree of virtualization increased. Connectedness to oneself, others, and the world was highest in reality, followed by MR and VR. For example, connectedness to oneself in reality had a mean of 66.253 (SD = 16.518) and a median of 67.833, compared to MR (M = 54.172, SD = 19.873) and VR (M = 54.871, SD = 15.165). Total connectedness scores followed a similar trend, with reality yielding the highest mean (M = 59.156, SD = 12.688) compared to MR (M = 45.125, SD = 10.116) and VR (M = 45.169, SD = 9.752).

Normality tests using the Shapiro-Wilk test showed that most paired differences adhered to a normal distribution ($p > 0.05$), allowing for the use of paired t-tests in hypothesis testing. For non-normally distributed variables, the Wilcoxon signed-rank test was applied to ensure statistical rigor. The results highlighted significant differences in connectedness between reality and both MR and VR across all dimensions, while comparisons between MR and VR revealed negligible differences.

The paired t-tests demonstrated that reality consistently yielded significantly higher connectedness scores than both MR and VR for all dimensions of connectedness. Table I summarizes the paired t-test results for the WCS variables. For connectedness to oneself, comparisons between reality and MR (t = 2.876, p = 0.007, Cohen's d = 0.517) and between reality and VR (t = 2.882, p = 0.007, Cohen's d = 0.518) revealed statistically significant differences, indicating a marked reduction in self-connectedness as virtualization increased. A similar trend was observed for connectedness to others, with reality scoring significantly higher than MR (t = 3.510, p = 0.001, Cohen's d = 0.630) and VR (t = 4.512, p < 0.001, Cohen's d = 0.810). The differences were most pronounced for connectedness to the world, where reality also outperformed both MR (t = 5.519, p < 0.001, Cohen's d = 0.991) and VR (t = 3.608, p = 0.001, Cohen's d = 0.648). The aggregated total connectedness scores mirrored these findings, with reality scoring significantly higher than MR (t = 5.798, p < 0.001, Cohen's d = 1.041) and VR (t = 5.321, p < 0.001, Cohen's d = 0.956).

These results demonstrate that reality offers a consistently higher degree of connectedness across all dimensions compared to MR and VR. The effect sizes (Cohen's d), ranging from moderate (0.517) to large (1.041), underscore the substantial impact of virtualization on reducing connectedness.

In stark contrast, no significant differences were found between MR and VR for any dimension of connectedness. The paired t-tests for total connectedness (t = -0.023, p = 0.982, Cohen's d = -0.004) and connectedness to oneself (t = -0.190, p = 0.851, Cohen's d = -0.034) revealed negligible effects. Wilcoxon signed-rank tests further supported these findings for non-normally distributed variables, such as connectedness to others (p = 0.565) and connectedness to the world (p = 0.276), where no significant differences were detected.

As a result, the alternative hypothesis (H_1) is only partially supported. While the degree of virtualization significantly affects connectedness when comparing reality to MR or VR, it does not do so between MR and VR.

The quantitative analysis of immersion and presence was conducted with 5 out of 31 participants under reality, MR, and VR conditions. The Shapiro-Wilk test indicated normality for 27 out of 36 variable pairs (p > 0.05). Paired t-tests showed significant differences in 2 of 15 presence pairs, with reality showing higher presence than MR, and in 1 of 21 immersion pairs, with VR showing higher immersion than reality. Wilcoxon signed-rank tests showed no significant differences across any pairs.

V. DISCUSSION

A. *Interpretation of Qualitative Results*

The qualitative analysis provided detailed insights into participants' subjective experiences across different reality forms.

Presence varied across settings. Real-world environments often fostered stronger presence due to physical interaction and sensory feedback. Participants described vivid memories and high attentiveness. In VR, presence depended on familiarity with the tasks and the VE. Some participants felt deeply immersed when the VE was realistic, while others reported lower presence due to difficulty engaging with the virtual scenario. In MR, presence combined real and virtual elements, offering advantages like familiarity through physical elements but also challenges, such as confusion about the nature of objects.

Immersion measures the depth of engagement in a scenario. VR offered the highest immersion, supported by its isolating nature and ability to create a sense of self-involvement in the VE [13]. Participants noted deep engagement during VR tasks, enhanced by the immersive design. MR had moderate immersion due to its mix of real and virtual elements, which sometimes caused confusion. Real-world environments provided physical interaction but were perceived as less challenging, leading to lower immersion.

Connectedness revealed notable differences between the environments. Real-world settings fostered the strongest emotional and physical connections. Watts et al. [7] describe self-connectedness as the integration of sensory, bodily, and emotional experiences. Participants in real environments reported a stronger connection to their senses and emotions than in VR or MR. Social connectedness was also highest in real settings, attributed to physical interactions and immediate feedback. In VR, isolation was common, while MR retained moderate connectedness by incorporating real-world elements. Connections to a greater purpose or nature were weakest in virtual environments, as participants found the artificial settings less meaningful.

B. Interpretation of Quantitative Results

Quantitative analysis examined connectedness (to self, others, and the world), presence, and immersion.

Watts et al. [23] emphasize the importance of sensory and emotional integration for self-connectedness. The lack of physical feedback in VR and MR might have contributed to the lower scores. Furthermore, cognitive dissonance caused by latency or visual artifacts in virtual environments could have hindered participants' ability to engage deeply with their senses and emotions.

Physical proximity and immediate feedback in these environments facilitated stronger interpersonal bonds, consistent with Watts et al.'s [23] framework, which describes social connectedness as a relational and structural concept. In VR and MR, the artificial nature of interactions may have limited participants' ability to build similar connections, and the absence of immediate physical feedback could have contributed to weaker social connectedness.

Connectedness to the world, including self-transcendence, purpose, and nature connection [23], was examined across environments. Differences in sensory and emotional input may influence the depth of experiences, with real-world scenarios offering a richer context compared to the reduced authenticity of virtual environments.

As was the case with previous expectations, presence and immersion showed no significant differences between reality forms, though VR tended to offer more immersive experiences, and real-world settings slightly higher presence. These trends could reflect the influence of task design and individual familiarity with the environments.

The results clearly support the hypothesis that real environments foster the highest levels of connectedness. However, the underlying reasons for these differences might lie in the sensory and emotional authenticity of real environments, which could have facilitated deeper engagement across all dimensions of connectedness. In contrast, MR and VR seem to have provided similar but less impactful experiences, as no significant differences were observed between these two settings. The lack of a clear pattern in presence and immersion was unexpected.

C. Contextualizing Connectedness

Watts et al. [23] highlight the multidimensional nature of connectedness, including self-awareness, social ties, and global purpose. Previous studies suggest XR technologies enhance connectedness through empathy-driven experiences. For example, Schutte and Stilinović [36] found VR scenarios, such as a refugee documentary, significantly increased empathy compared to 2D media. Herrera et al. [37] demonstrated that VR experiences of homelessness foster long-lasting positive attitudes and increased social engagement. Additionally, Deighan et al. [38] explored VRChat as a tool for supporting social connectedness and well-being, highlighting the platform's potential for mental health support. Similarly, Thabrew et al. [39] reported that immersive experiences could reduce social isolation and improve connectedness among hospitalized children and young people.

The concept of self-connectedness is also well-supported in VR research. Ganschow et al. [5] observed that perspective-taking exercises in VR enhanced self-continuity and emotional connection to one's future self.

Connectedness to the world, specifically to nature, can also be enhanced through VR. Leung et al. [41] found that exposure to nature in immersive VR increased individuals' connectedness to nature, particularly among those with low affinity for natural environments. Additionally, Stepanova et al. [40] noted that VR simulations of the "Overview Effect"—a phenomenon experienced by astronauts viewing Earth from space—can evoke a profound sense of global connectedness and environmental responsibility.

These studies demonstrate XR's potential to enhance connectedness. However, when comparisons are made, they are typically limited to traditional media or conventional methods, such as perspective-taking exercises, empathy-building tasks, or self-reflection activities, rather than directly contrasting XR with real-world experiences. This limitation highlights the need for further research directly comparing XR and real environments.

D. Implications

In education, the empirical findings indicate that the strongest connectedness was observed in real environments, suggesting a substantiated prioritization of real interactions in learning settings to enhance the sense of connectedness. Strategies to enhance connectedness in virtual environments are crucial, focusing on methods such as fostering physical feedback mechanisms or incorporating real-world elements.

In healthcare, MR can enhance the effectiveness of medical education, training, diagnosis, and treatment, as well as strengthen doctor-patient relationships [42]. However, the study also demonstrated isolation effects in pure VR applications, highlighting the need for measures to mitigate these effects to improve therapeutic outcomes.

The results also underscore the necessity of addressing the reduced connectedness experienced by general consumers in XR technologies to safeguard their emotional well-being.

No significant differences in presence and immersion were found between VR, MR, and real environments, suggesting that VR and MR can offer comparable experiences. Further research is needed to address limitations in fostering emotional and social connectedness.

E. Limitations

This study faced several limitations that should be considered when interpreting the results.

The sample size and composition posed a key limitation. While the qualitative sample included 5 participants and the quantitative sample 31, these numbers might be insufficient for drawing generalizable conclusions. Although demographic diversity was ensured, future studies with larger and more varied samples could enhance the robustness of findings.

A notable methodological limitation was the design of scenarios for the virtualization levels. Despite careful replication, these tasks did not reflect typical use cases, potentially limiting the authenticity and applicability of MR and VR experiences to real-world scenarios.

In the quantitative analysis, standard introduction applications were used to ensure representative MR and VR experiences. However, these applications differed between conditions, restricting direct comparability. For instance, real-world experiences relied on participants recalling past events, which significantly depended on the nature of the memories themselves. This reliance may have influenced the comparability with MR and VR scenarios, as the type and context of the recalled memory could impact the measured variables. With more resources, improved research designs could potentially have led to more robust findings.

Another limitation was the absence of social interaction in the connectedness measurements. Scenarios lacked interaction with other users, reducing the ability to assess social connectedness. While efforts were made to cover all aspects of connectedness, resource constraints unfortunately limited the ability to address each aspect equally well. Future studies should include social components for a more comprehensive understanding of connectedness.

The use of the WCS scale introduced another constraint. Originally developed for general connectedness and validated in contexts such as psychedelic experiences [7], the WCS was not specifically designed for VR and MR. This limitation may have prevented it from capturing nuanced aspects of connectedness unique to these environments.

The quantitative analysis used limited statistical methods; additional techniques such as ANOVA or MANOVA could have provided deeper insights into variable relationships, especially if demographic factors were included.

Several factors, suggested by prior research as potentially influencing VR and MR experiences, were not examined in this study.

Consequently, claims regarding XR's impact on connectedness should be made cautiously until sufficient empirical evidence supports them.

VI. Conclusion and Future Work

A. *Conclusion*

This study provided significant insights into VR and MR research, particularly concerning connectedness, presence, and immersion. The qualitative analysis explored how XR environments are perceived regarding these variables, while the quantitative analysis examined the impact of virtualization levels on perceived connectedness, focusing on self, others, and the world.

Findings revealed no consistent significant differences in presence and immersion between VR, MR, and real environments. However, connectedness was found to be stronger in real environments compared to VR and MR, partially confirming the hypothesis that the degree of virtualization influences connectedness. The absence of significant differences between VR and MR suggests that these technologies may affect connectedness in similar ways, with physical presence and sensory stimuli likely being key factors for fostering connectedness.

These findings emphasize the importance of real-world sensory stimuli and physical presence for connectedness while highlighting VR and MR's potential as less intensive alternatives. Prior research indicates that VR and MR can enhance connectedness when replacing empathy-focused tasks, but caution is warranted when these technologies substitute real-world experiences, as they may reduce connectedness. By directly comparing these technologies with real environments, this study contributes to understanding their social and psychological impacts.

The practical applications of these findings are diverse. The strong connectedness observed in real environments suggests that educational settings should prioritize real interactions. In cases where physical presence is not possible, MR and VR can be effective alternatives, provided strategies are implemented to address the lower levels of connectedness typically found in virtual environments.

Given the widespread use of VR, AR, and MR in industries such as gaming, healthcare, and education, addressing connectedness is essential for user well-being. Research shows that connectedness to self, others, and the world is often significantly lower in VR and MR. Measures should be taken to understand and mitigate potential negative effects on emotional well-being, particularly in therapeutic contexts where a lack of connectedness could hinder treatment outcomes.

The study also suggests that VR and MR can achieve levels of presence comparable to real-world settings, opening new possibilities in training, education, and therapy without concerns about perceived presence. Similarly, immersion effects in VR and MR are comparable to those in real environments, making these technologies suitable for applications requiring deep engagement.

However, the study faced limitations. The small sample size may limit the generalizability of results. The absence of social interactions in measuring connectedness and the use of the WCS, which was not specifically designed for VR and MR, further constrained the findings.

This study makes valuable contributions to VR and MR research, demonstrating how these technologies influence connectedness, presence, and immersion. The findings hold practical relevance for education, therapy, and entertainment while forming a foundation for future studies to further explore and expand these insights. While VR and MR offer numerous benefits, their potential to create new realities that influence connectedness must be critically examined to ensure their use delivers positive outcomes without unintended negative effects.

B. *Future Work*

Several areas for future research remain to deepen and expand the findings of this study. Future studies should incorporate larger and more diverse samples to enhance the generalizability of results. Utilizing advanced data analytics platforms could facilitate this process. Including participants from varied demographic groups could provide valuable insights, as connectedness, presence, and immersion may be experienced differently across populations. This is particularly important given the limited research comparing VR and MR environments to real-world settings.

Further exploration of specific variables, such as the long-term effects of VR and MR experiences, is needed. Wearable technology could help track these over time. Examining how connectedness, presence, and immersion evolve over time could reveal the sustainability of these effects. Methodological improvements, such as refining and validating the WCS for VR and MR contexts, could enhance the accuracy of future studies. VR platforms with built-in tools can streamline this process. Additionally, new or supplementary methods could provide richer data and better address the unique challenges of these environments.

Practical applications of these findings in education, therapy, and industry warrant further investigation. Developing interventions based on these results could improve the effectiveness and usability of VR and MR technologies. AI-driven social interactions could enhance realism. Integrating social interactions in VR and MR environments may improve the measurement of social connectedness and provide more realistic application scenarios.

Longitudinal studies are needed to assess the long-term stability and application of these findings. Regular monitoring of connectedness, presence, and immersion over time could offer a more comprehensive understanding of their progression. Interdisciplinary collaboration could bring new perspectives and foster innovative approaches by involving experts from psychology, sociology, and computer science.

Finally, social and cultural factors should be examined to understand their impact on VR and MR experiences. Adapting research to various cultural and social contexts could increase the generalizability and relevance of findings. Leveraging international research networks could be beneficial. Exploring emerging technologies and methods since this study could also enhance future research, enabling greater accuracy and applicability of results.

Acknowledgment

This work was supervised by Prof. Dr. Karsten Huffstadt and Prof. Dr. habil. Nicholas Müller from the Faculty of Computer Science and Business Information Systems, University of Applied Sciences Würzburg-Schweinfurt.

References

[1] J.-C. Servotte et al., "Virtual reality experience: Immersion, sense of presence, and cybersickness," Clinical Simulation in Nursing, vol. 38, pp. 35–43, Jan. 2020, doi: 10.1016/j.ecns.2019.09.006.

[2] C. Flavian, S. Ibáñez Sánchez, and C. Orús, "The impact of virtual, augmented and mixed reality technologies on the customer experience," Journal of Business Research, pp. 547–560, Nov. 2018, doi: 10.1016/j.jbusres.2018.10.050.

[3] E. Lemle, K. Bomkamp, M. K. Williams, and E. Cutbirth, "Virtual Reality and the Future of Entertainment," in Two Bit Circus and the Future of Entertainment, E. Lemle, K. Bomkamp, M. K. Williams, and E. Cutbirth, Eds., Cham: Springer International Publishing, 2015, pp. 25–37. doi: 10.1007/978-3-319-25793-8_4.

[4] F. Ke, S. Lee, and X. Xu, "Teaching training in a mixed-reality integrated learning environment," Computers in Human Behavior, vol. 62, pp. 212–220, Sep. 2016, doi: 10.1016/j.chb.2016.03.094.

[5] B. Ganschow, L. Cornet, S. Zebel, and J.-L. van Gelder, "Looking Back From the Future: Perspective Taking in Virtual Reality Increases Future Self-Continuity," Front. Psychol., vol. 12, pp. 1–11, Jun. 2021, doi: 10.3389/fpsyg.2021.664687.

[6] J. Hvass et al., "Visual realism and presence in a virtual reality game," in 2017 3DTV Conference: The True Vision - Capture, Transmission and Display of 3D Video (3DTV-CON), Jun. 2017, pp. 1–4. doi: 10.1109/3DTV.2017.8280421.

[7] R. Watts et al., "The Watts Connectedness Scale: a new scale for measuring a sense of connectedness to self, others, and world," Psychopharmacology, vol. 239, no. 11, pp. 3461–3483, Nov. 2022, doi: 10.1007/s00213-022-06187-5.

[8] K. Klussman, N. Curtin, J. Langer, and A. L. Nichols, "The Importance of Awareness, Acceptance, and Alignment With the Self: A Framework for Understanding Self-Connection," Europe's Journal of Psychology, vol. 18, no. 1, pp. 120–131, Feb. 2022, doi: 10.5964/ejop.3707.

[9] D. T. van Bel, K. C. H. J. Smolders, W. A. IJsselsteijn, and Y. a. W. De Kort, "Social connectedness: concept and measurement," in Intelligent Environments 2009, IOS Press, 2009, pp. 67–74. doi: 10.3233/978-1-60750-034-6-67.

[10] K. Pavlovich and K. Krahnke, "Empathy, Connectedness and Organisation," J Bus Ethics, vol. 105, no. 1, pp. 131–137, Jan. 2012, doi: 10.1007/s10551-011-0961-3.

[11] C. R. Phillips-Salimi, J. E. Haase, and W. Carter Kooken, "Connectedness in the context of patient–provider relationships:a concept analysis," Journal of Advanced Nursing, vol. 68, pp. 230–245, Jul. 2011, doi: 10.1111/j.1365-2648.2011.05763.x.

[12] M. Slater and S. Wilbur, "A Framework for Immersive Virtual Environments (FIVE): Speculations on the Role of Presence in Virtual Environments," Presence: Teleoperators & Virtual Environments, vol. 6, no. 6, pp. 603–616, Dec. 1997, doi: 10.1162/pres.1997.6.6.603.

[13] B. G. Witmer and M. J. Singer, "Measuring Presence in Virtual Environments: A Presence Questionnaire," Presence: Teleoperators and Virtual Environments, vol. 7, no. 3, pp. 225–240, Jun. 1998, doi: 10.1162/105474698565686.

[14] M. Slater, "Place Illusion and Plausibility Can Lead to Realistic Behaviour in Immersive Virtual Environments," Philosophical transactions of the Royal Society of London. Series B, Biological sciences, vol. 364, pp. 3549–57, Dec. 2009, doi: 10.1098/rstb.2009.0138.

[15] M. Slater et al., "A Separate Reality: An Update on Place Illusion and Plausibility in Virtual Reality," Frontiers in Virtual Reality, vol. 3, p. 914392, Jun. 2022, doi: 10.3389/frvir.2022.914392.

[16] M. Slater, "Immersion and the illusion of presence in virtual reality," British Journal of Psychology, vol. 109, pp. 431–433, Mar. 2018, doi: 10.1111/bjop.12305.

[17] S. Agrawal, A. Simon, S. Bech, K. Bærentsen, and S. Forchhammer, "Defining Immersion: Literature Review and Implications for Research on Audiovisual Experiences," Audio Engineering Society (AES) Convention, vol. 68, no. 6, pp. 404–417, Oct. 2019, doi: https://doi.org/10.17743/jaes.2020.0039.

[18] N. C. Nilsson, R. Nordahl, and S. Serafin, "Immersion Revisited: A Review of Existing Definitions of Immersion and Their Relation to Different Theories of Presence," Human Technology: An Interdisciplinary Journal on Humans in ICT Environments, vol. 12, no. 2, pp. 108–134, Nov. 2016, doi: http://dx.doi.org/10.17011/ht/urn.201611174652.

[19] S. A. Smith and N. W. Mulligan, "Immersion, presence, and episodic memory in virtual reality environments," Memory, vol. 29, no. 8, pp. 983–1005, Sep. 2021, doi: 10.1080/09658211.2021.1953535.

[20] J. Mütterlein, "The Three Pillars of Virtual Reality? Investigating the Roles of Immersion, Presence, and Interactivity," in Proceedings of the 51st Hawaii International Conference on System Sciences, Hawaii, USA: Hawaii International Conference on System Sciences (HICSS), Jan. 2018, pp. 1407–1415. doi: 10.24251/HICSS.2018.174.

[21] M. P. McCreery, P. G. Schrader, S. K. Krach, and R. Boone, "A sense of self: The role of presence in virtual environments," Computers in Human Behavior, vol. 29, no. 4, pp. 1635–1640, Jul. 2013, doi: 10.1016/j.chb.2013.02.002.

[22] G. W. Young, N. O'Dwyer, and A. Smolic, "Exploring virtual reality for quality immersive empathy building experiences," Behaviour & Information Technology, vol. 41, no. 16, pp. 3415–3431, Dec. 2022, doi: 10.1080/0144929X.2021.1993336.

[23] R. Watts et al., "Watts Connectedness Scale (WCS)." Nov. 01, 2022. [Online]. Available: https://static1.squarespace.com/static/61d19cb24fa60d0025184c88/t/62f0f5e309f3060a33465b65/1659958755640/Final+WCS_manual-docx-1.pdf. [Retrieved: February, 2025].

[24] M. Usoh, E. Catena, S. Arman, and M. Slater, "Slater-Usoh-Steed Presence," Slater-Usoh-Steed Presence. Accessed: Jul. 12, 2024. [Online]. Available: https://ashleyoiknine.wixsite.com/ashleyoiknine/copy-of-immersive-tendency-question-1. [Retrieved: February, 2025].

[25] K. Tcha-Tokey, O. Christmann, E. Loup-Escande, and S. Richir, "Proposition and Validation of a Questionnaire to Measure the User Experience in Immersive Virtual Environments," The International Journal of Virtual Reality, vol. 16, pp. 33–48, Oct. 2016, doi: 10.20870/IJVR.2016.16.1.2880.

[26] VR Compare, "Meta Quest 3: Full Specification," VRcompare. Accessed: Aug. 16, 2024. [Online]. Available: https://vr-compare.com/headset/metaquest3. [Retrieved: February, 2025].

[27] VR Compare, "Oculus Rift S: Full Specification," VRcompare. Accessed: Aug. 16, 2024. [Online]. Available: https://vr-compare.com/headset/oculusrifts. [Retrieved: February, 2025].

[28] Unity, "Real-time development platform from Unity | 3D, 2D, VR and AR engine," Unity. Accessed: Jul. 02, 2024. [Online]. Available: https://unity.com/. [Retrieved: February, 2025].

[29] Sketchfab, "Features," Sketchfab. Accessed: Jul. 11, 2024. [Online]. Available: https://sketchfab.com/features. [Retrieved: February, 2025].

[30] Steam, "Figmin XR - Tilt Five on Steam." Accessed: Jul. 02, 2024. [Online]. Available: https://store.steampowered.com/app/1890220/Figmin_XR__Tilt_Five/. [Retrieved: February, 2025].

[31] S. Misoch, Qualitative Interviews. De Gruyter Oldenbourg, 2014. doi: 10.1515/9783110354614.

[32] Meta, "First Encounters for Meta Quest | Quest VR Games | Meta Store." Accessed: Jul. 19, 2024. [Online]. Available: https://www.meta.com/de-de/experiences/6236169136472090/. [Retrieved: February, 2025].

[33] Meta, "Oculus First Contact on Meta Quest," Oculus. [Online]. Available: https://www.meta.com/experiences/quest/2188021891257542/. [Retrieved: February, 2025].

[34] GlobalData, "Virtual Reality Market Size, Share and Trends Analysis Report by End-User Type (Enterprise, Consumer), IT Infrastructure (Hardware, Software) and Region (North America, Europe, Asia Pacific, Central & South America, Middle East & Africa) and Segment Forecast to 2030," Market Research Reports & Consulting | GlobalData UK Ltd. Accessed: Jul. 19, 2024. [Online]. Available: https://www.globaldata.com/store/report/vr-market-analysis/. [Retrieved: February, 2025].

[35] "JASP - A Fresh Way to Do Statistics," JASP - Free and User-Friendly Statistical Software. Accessed: Nov. 20, 2024. [Online]. Available: https://jasp-stats.org/. [Retrieved: February, 2025].

[36] N. S. Schutte and E. J. Stilinović, "Facilitating empathy through virtual reality," Motiv Emot, vol. 41, no. 6, pp. 708–712, Dec. 2017, doi: 10.1007/s11031-017-9641-7.

[37] F. Herrera, J. Bailenson, E. Weisz, E. Ogle, and J. Zaki, "Building long-term empathy: A large-scale comparison of traditional and virtual reality perspective-taking," PLOS ONE, vol. 13, no. 10, p. e0204494, Oct. 2018, doi: 10.1371/journal.pone.0204494.

[38] M. T. Deighan, A. Ayobi, and A. A. O'Kane, "Social Virtual Reality as a Mental Health Tool: 2023 CHI Conference on Human Factors in Computing Systems, CHI 2023," CHI 2023 - Proceedings of the 2023 CHI Conference on Human Factors in Computing Systems, Apr. 2023, doi: 10.1145/3544548.3581103.

[39] H. Thabrew, L. A. Chubb, H. Kumar, and C. Fouché, "Immersive Reality Experience Technology for Reducing Social Isolation and Improving Social Connectedness and Well-being of Children and Young People Who Are Hospitalized: Open Trial," JMIR Pediatr Parent, vol. 5, no. 1, p. e29164, Mar. 2022, doi: 10.2196/29164.

[40] E. Stepanova, D. Quesnel, and B. Riecke, "Space-A Virtual Frontier: How to Design and Evaluate a Virtual Reality Experience of the Overview Effect," Frontiers in Digital Humanities, vol. 6, Apr. 2019, doi: 10.3389/fdigh.2019.00007.

[41] G. Leung, H. Hazan, and C. Chan, "Exposure to nature in immersive virtual reality increases connectedness to nature among people with low nature affinity," Journal of Environmental Psychology, vol. 83, p. 101863, Aug. 2022, doi: 10.1016/j.jenvp.2022.101863.

[42] M.-C. Hsieh and J.-J. Lee, "Preliminary Study of VR and AR Applications in Medical and Healthcare Education," Journal of Nursing and Health Studies, vol. 3, no. 1, pp. 1–5, Feb. 2018, doi: 10.21767/2574-2825.100030.

Intergenerational Codesign of Immersive Technology for a Heritage Site and Underwater VR Experience

Marius N. Varga[1], Oksana Hagen[2], Rory Baxter[3], Alejandro Veliz Reyes[1], Ray B Jones[3], Amir Aly[2], Dena Bazazian[2], Swen Gaudl[4]
[1]School of Art, Design and Architecture, University of Plymouth, UK
[2]School of Engineering, Computing and Mathematics, University of Plymouth, UK
[3]School of Nursing and Midwifery, University of Plymouth, UK
[4]Department of Applied IT, div CLIC, University of Gothenburg, Sweden
e-mail: {marius.varga | oksana.hagen | rory.baxter | alejandro.velizreyes | ray.jones | amir.aly | dena.bazazian}@plymouth.ac.uk; swen.gaudl@ait.gu.se

Abstract—**The development of immersive Extended Reality (XR) applications tailored for older adults remains a significant challenge, even amidst rapid technological advancements. Neglecting to account for the specific needs and requirements of end-users in the design process can result in reduced adoption rates or a total lack of engagement. We present findings and recommendations for building immersive experiences for older adults by exploring the similarities and differences encountered during the development of two immersive XR applications, with a specific focus on cultural heritage and underwater telepresence. The application development followed a monthly, iterative approach, integrating rapid prototyping for a total of 16 intergenerational codesign workshops, with 24 older adults and 12 younger adults codesign participants. The findings indicate that immersive experiences for older adults have significant potential to effectively recreate cultural heritage sites or underwater environments in XR. However, achieving this requires the implementation of simplified and intuitive locomotion and interaction mechanisms, facilitated through a streamlined and simplified control scheme. In addition, accessibility and affordability together with comfort in using the immersive hardware and minimising hand strain when holding the controllers are priorities for older age codesign participants.**

Keywords-xr; intergenerational codesign; heritage; underwater; digital exclusion.

I. Introduction

Advances in immersive technology such as Extended Reality (XR) have opened the door to new opportunities creating novel ways of accessing an engaging with museums and heritage sites [1]. Evidence suggests that younger audiences prefer Virtual Reality (VR) as a learning environment for cultural heritage [2]. This does not imply technological exclusion for older audiences, it highlights the need to go beyond usability testing and consider their interests and requirements for newly created content [3]. Although younger audiences are potentially drawn to the novelty and interactivity of VR, older audiences might engage more deeply with content that resonates with their life experiences and memories.

Through the Intergenerational Codesign of Novel Technologies In Coastal Communities (ICONIC) project, our aim was to give codesign participants (contributors), both young and old, a voice in the creation process and help them integrate their needs, suggestions and requirements into the design of novel technologies. The general aim of the ICONIC project was to develop four novel technologies through intergenerational codesign that would help connect digitally disadvantaged older people to local heritage and the environment. From the expertise of our team and our coastal context, we had nominated four general areas of technology: extended reality for heritage, underwater telepresence, social games, and voice-AI over the telephone. This paper will focus on the intergenerational codesign approach to develop a Heritage Extended Reality (HXR) application and an Underwater Telepresence (UT) application. In the rest of the paper, we will refer to heritage extended reality as HXR and Underwater Telepresence as UT and any Extended Reality concepts and terms as XR.

Ijaz et al. [4] highlighted ten categories of design considerations for older adults that focused on users and physical configuration, hardware usage and the design of the immersive application. Through our codesign process we had the opportunity to address the majority of the categories such as: *onboarding and assistance* through supplementary sessions in order to familiarise the contributors with the hardware and the concept of VR; *safety* with support for contributors to explore VR standing or sitting in the presence of a researcher; *visuals* designed and created to capture the sense of being the physical heritage site; *audio* with the implementation of spatial audio; *personalisation* customisation of the VR headset and the controllers to help users with reduced mobility; *usability* with custom interaction metaphors for engaging with the virtual environment; *engagement* adding a gamified experience through interaction with historical artefacts; *minimise side effects* through support and clear instructions especially when testing new control mappings or unique locomotion techniques. *Embodiment* was addressed through the implementation of localised walking complemented by teleportation. In addition, it also includes automatic adjustment of the user's height when they put on the VR headset although we did not use an avatar to represent the user's body. *Realism* was addressed using actual measurements to recreate the heritage site in virtual space combined with ambient sounds. Throughout this paper, we will unpack the elements that contributed to each category in more detail.

This paper demonstrates how intergenerational codesign not only enriches the engagement of older adults with immersive

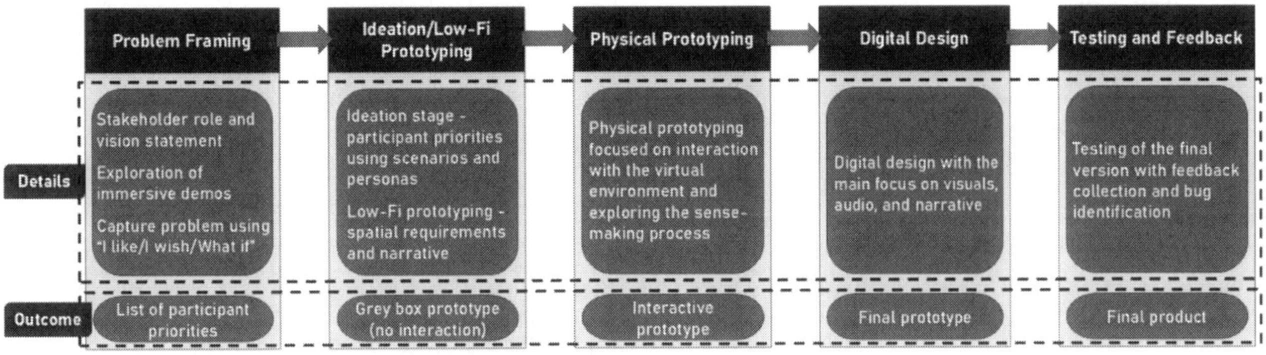

Figure 1. Timeline for the HXR and UT work package. The timeline is split in five distinct stages with an approximate one month duration for each stage. This approach is common to all ICONIC's work packages.

technologies but also crucially informs the development of accessible and intuitive user interfaces in cultural heritage and underwater environments. By integrating extensive user feedback into the design process, we offer novel insights into creating more inclusive and effective immersive experiences.

The remainder of the paper is structured as follows. Section II provides a background and overview of our approach to codesign in the ICONIC project including the exploratory aspect of technology development. Section III describes the methodology and approach in the implementation of the project with a focus on contributors recruitment, partner involvement, and the iterative development process that integrates feedback from the codesign team. Section IV explores the outcome for each package, focusing on the immersive application for each package, and highlighting additional recommendations and findings. Section V provides a discussion of common elements in packages and also highlights some of the differences between them. Section VI draws the conclusions of the article and highlights future work.

This project approaches codesign from a participatory perspective, accessing the dormant creative potential of intergenerational groups through hands-on creative methods including storytelling and experience design, technology development, and interaction design. Here, the project has followed precedent from prior research [5] suggesting ten principles to codesign XR experiences for health interventions in rural communities [6], allowing end users to envision future and speculative scenarios (in this case, shaped by engaging with a local heritage location), the delivery of a research-in-residence approach [7], and the contextualization of XR design within defined societal groups and geographies, among others. These guidelines stem mainly from the GOALD project [8], which focused on physical activity and reminiscence and included a menu of XR experiences for further evaluation and feedback from older adults groups. In addition to those results emerging from the participation of older adults, we pose the question of whether rural communities can benefit from the creative participation of young people in need of high-value digital skills. Furthermore, the literature [9] [10] indicates that youth disenfranchisement results in more critical social outcomes, e.g. vulnerability, mental health and isolation, and feelings of 'nowhere to go'.

Heritage sites and museums play a vital role in the lives of many individuals, particularly in rural communities across South-West England. A 2018 UK Government report examined the influence of historic sites on wellbeing and one of the highlights is the concept of "Heritage as Place" [11]. The report, emphasises the importance of belonging, where the connection to historic locations contributes to reduced social isolation and strengthens feelings of pride, identity, and community. However, these advantages are not experienced equally across all segments of society, with older generation visitors experiencing accessibility and mobility issues. From a large partner network of 36 organisations [12], we partnered with Cotehele - National Trust to create a digital immersive version of the heritage site. Cotehele is a historic estate located in Cornwall, England, and features a medieval manor house, gardens, and a mill. The Great Hall, a significant architectural point of interest of Cotehele, was constructed in the late 15th century and has been preserved in traditional Georgian style for centuries.

With Ocean Conservation Trust (OCT), Plymouth, England, as a partner for the UT work package, the ICONIC project explores how these immersive tools can bridge physical and financial barriers, providing access to the otherwise inaccessible underwater world. Inspired by the beneficial effects of blue spaces on well-being [13], our goal is to simulate an underwater experience, enabling people onshore to explore marine environments that are otherwise out of reach. The codesign workshops centered on designing an interaction with the marine environment to evoke a sense of "being underwater" while addressing the practical challenges associated with such a design. The concept of telepresence — originally introduced in human-computer interaction to describe the illusion of being present in a distant location — has evolved beyond its technical roots. Sheridan [14] describes telepresence as the sensation of being "there" at a remote site. Within the scope of the ICONIC project, we have adopted a broader phenomenological view emphasising the sense of presence in underwater spaces that could include methods such as VR and pre-recorded content, enabling engagement without real-time telecommunication [15].

In line with design thinking, we have started the development from the first principles, by understanding what is it that stands out the most about the heritage sites and underwater spaces to our codesign participants and what are the main barriers to higher levels of engagement with these spaces. The goal of the project was to allow contributors to explore different modalities of immersion and interaction and to allow them to define what it means to experience a heritage or underwater spaces in an immersive environment. The technical solutions differ in a way they are delivered and in the resulting level of accessibility, interactivity and immersion for both packages.

II. Methodology

The ICONIC project recruited twelve Digitally Excluded Older People (DEOP) aged 50+ for the HXR workshop group, and a further twelve DEOP for the UT workshop group. Six Young People (YP) were recruited for the HXR, and an additional six YP were recruited for the UT group. Attendance amongst the younger cohort for both groups was more inconsistent than amongst DEOP contributors. To support asynchronous codesign an additional group of 20 YP were recruited through a higher education partner of the ICONIC project. The project received approval from the Ethics Committee of the University of Plymouth and each contributor received an information sheet and offered the option to withdraw from the study at any time. After each workshop, the contributors were encouraged to raise any issues or provide feedback in person and anonymously through a suggestion box. For analysis, data was anonymised and kept secure on the University of Plymouth machine and OneDrive protected by passwords. Access to the data was limited to the ICONIC team. Codesign participants and partner organisations have given permission for the photos used in this article.

The development process was created to reflect the contributors' involvement at different stages of the codesign process. The five main stages are as follows: Problem Framing, Ideation, Physical prototyping, Digital Design and Testing and Feedback, as described in Figure 1.

Each workshop followed a four-step iterative design approach as described by Macklin and Sharp [16]: Conceptualise, Prototype, Playtest and Evaluation. In the Concept phase - The research team will generate the concepts that it wanted to explore next based on the current development stage of the application and the feedback received. Prototype phase - the concepts get transferred into codesign activities and a technical prototype gets created. The playtest phase - during the workshop the codesign team generates feedback and knowledge through testing the prototypes and executing the designated activities. Evaluation phase - after the workshop the research team evaluates the workshop results, both from activities and the prototype feedback, and generates a new set of concepts to explore for the next workshop. This approach was applied to both the HXR package and the UT package as described by Jones et al. [12]. There were similarities in data collection between the two work packages, as the focus of each was understanding contributors' needs and design priorities for the two technologies. Each workshop featured a variety of activities that were designed to produce written or verbal feedback to support the iterative design of the technologies (Figure 2). Workshop materials and audio recordings were cleaned and transcribed verbatim for thematic analysis.

Figure 2. During the co-design session, participants prototyped immersive interactions by annotating paper templates of 360° environments, taking snapshots, and instantly exploring their work in Google Cardboard VR. This iterative approach promoted deeper understanding and collaboration.

With Cotehele as a partner for the HXR, contributors chose from a set of six possible indoor locations part of the Cotehele's manor by using 360-degree videos captured at each location. The codesign team selected the Great Hall (Figure 3) due to its impressive size and extensive range of historical artefacts on display, although other locations, such as the kitchen, had great potential in exploring novel and immersive interactions.

For the UT, as contributors prioritized local marine environments early on, we focused on prototyping the interaction with the footage from two National Marine Aquarium (NMA) Plymouth tanks dedicated to local fauna and flora: Plymouth Sound and Eddystone reef. The prototype leveraged 360-degree camera footage, Oculus Quest headset [17] and artificial intelligence (AI) for interactive species identification (implemented as an OpenAI API placeholder for the time being). A point-and-click interaction method was selected based on contributors' feedback, with the option to scroll through the menu and the collection of species. The features of the prototype make it suitable for deployment in care homes, schools, and even tourism hubs, offering a scalable model for broad outreach and engagement.

III. Outcome

Although both packages have an immersive experience as the primary outcome, there are other secondary aspects that emerged as a result of the codesign workshops.

Figure 3. Image taken inside the Great Hall in Cotehele - National Trust UK.

A. Heritage XR

1) Multimodal immersive experience: The main outcome of the HXR package is an immersive VR experience replicating the Cotehele's Great Hall (see the image on the left in Figure 4). The application is a multisensory experience that makes use of visual, audio and haptic feedback. The VR is delivered using the Quest 2 headset developed by Meta [18], which includes two VR controllers. The headset features six degrees of freedom (6DoF) using an inside-out tracking system and is equipped with a set of speakers that allows the delivery of 3-dimensional sound. The tracked controllers support 6DoF and have customisable buttons and haptic feedback capabilities. The virtual space has been created using a combination of local textures, rough measurements, and recreation of the main features of the hall. A set of 4 unique historical artefacts have been scanned using Photogrammetry [19] and due to limited resources and time constraints, the rest of the artefacts in the Great Hall are 3D digital replicas of weapons and items acquired through the Unreal Engine asset store [20].

2) Technical prototype with simplified interactions aimed at older adults: The codesign process revealed the challenges older adults face with various metaphors of interaction, found in most VR applications. Therefore, a set of simplified interactions were created aimed at alleviating some of the issues, such as holding a button pressed for a long time or hard-to-reach buttons. A combination of button mapping and interactive objects was packaged in an example project in Unreal Engine [21]. The interactive elements are modular and flexible, and developers can turn any asset into an interactive object.

3) UX recommendation for the development of VR applications: A set of recommendations for the development of a technical immersive application for older adults through an intergenerational codesign approach. These recommendations are in the process of being published soon in a peer reviewed article.

B. Underwater Telepresence

There are three outcomes from the UT codesign sessions:

1) Immersive Prototype: The main outcome is the immersive VR prototype designed to include most of the features designed by our contributors. There are two modes of interaction: "learning" and "relaxation". Relaxation is designed for users seeking a calming experience; this mode emphasizes the serene beauty of the underwater world with ambient sounds and minimal distractions. The learning (or stimulating) mode enables users to interact and identify marine species within the immersive environment. Features such as "collecting" fish and a virtual agent, designed as a friendly "penguin," engage users with contextual challenges to encourage users to explore the space more actively. Feedback emphasized the need for realistic, but not necessarily real sound, with ambient underwater sounds enhancing immersion.

2) Design of Alternative Delivery Modes: While there was general agreement about the use of the VR headset, the contributors proposed additional modes of delivery of the experience. The proposed design included a web interface with the ability to interact with 360-degree underwater footage in the same way as before, use of a large interactive screen (that was used to demonstrate the live video in Workshop 2), emphasising the social interaction aspect as an important part of the design. One of the alternative designs to the headset included a portable mini-dome. While the dome enabled shared experiences, it was deemed to be less immersive compared to headsets and limited in scalability due to the infrastructure required. In all design decisions, contributors prioritised accessibility and scalability above most other design properties.

3) Established Feasibility of Using ROV for Outreach: Remote Operated Vehicles (ROVs) emerged as a promising outreach tool, offering a hands-on, interactive modality to experience underwater environments. We tested the feasibility of the ROV-based telepresence project in an outdoor setting, allowing contributors to directly engage in marine exploration. The contributors operated the ROV, navigating an underwater outdoor space in real-time. To improve the comfort of contributors, we have also offered one-to-one ROV teleoperation training sessions in the indoor pool. Throughout the workshop, contributors expressed interest in extending interactivity through robotic arms for activities such as object collection or habitat observation.

IV. Discussion

The generalist approach taken in the development of HXR and UT offered a unique opportunity to explore multiple directions and delivery methods for the experience. Rather than narrowing the scope early, the projects deliberately kept the solution space broad, enabling the team to investigate a variety of technologies and approaches. For HXR, our initial findings identified similar challenges to Wu et al. [22], with older adults experiencing difficulties, such as headset-related neck fatigue and limited field of view leading to extra head

Figure 4. On the left, HXR - final version of the Cotehele's Great Hall aiming to capture the unique "look and feel" from inside the great hall. On the right, UT. An example of interaction with the 360-degree footage of the underwater environment.

movement leading to decreased motor performance. Therefore, the interaction and locomotion were prioritiesed by the codesign team to improve accessibility and direct interaction. For the UT the focus was on exploring various methods of allowing contributors to experience telepresence through controlled ROVs and recorded underwater environments in VR. This exploratory strategy revealed new possibilities and improved the understanding of what users value in such an experience. However, this openness also posed challenges, highlighting the need for technical expertise and resources, and limiting the final application to a prototype.

Accessibility emerged as a decisive factor in nearly every stage of the project. Whether considering the mobility of devices, their cost, or ease of use, the contributors consistently emphasized the importance of making the technology as inclusive as possible. For instance, while immersive dome projections offered an interesting social dynamic, they were ultimately de-prioritized due to their high infrastructure requirements and limited portability. For both packages, the headset with the lowest price was chosen by the contributors to increase accessibility. These decisions reinforced the need to prioritize technologies that could reach the largest audience, even if it meant compromising certain experiential features.

A. *Exploration through technology interaction*

The ability to explore through interaction was one of the key factors that the codesign team highlighted early in the process in both the HXR and UT packages. Workshop 1 was dedicated to problem framing, the contributors explored technologies dedicated to each package in order to identify the key elements of an immersive heritage and underwater telepresence experience

For HXR, some key elements highlighted by the team were: (i) accessing heritage information through novel and unique ways such as a non-player character (NPC) that provides information about the various historical artefacts; (ii) collaboration between two or more users in exploring the digital space; and (iii) education and knowledge through gamified experiences such as an escape-the-room puzzle.

The exploratory aspect of the codesign process combined with the onboarding sessions and equipment support [23] from the researchers provided contributors with a unique opportunity to explore both the limitations and possibilities inherent in technology, leading to a deeper understanding, reduced cognitive load and reducing their initial reluctance to engage. This was evidenced by the preferences for movement in the VR environment. Initially, teleportation as the initial locomotion metaphor, proved challenging for some of the contributors. A combination of controls and the ability to aim towards a landing spot made some contributors uncomfortable. A more simple locomotion, called "grab-and-drag" was initially preferred, but as the contributors became more experienced with the VR technology, they started to revert to the teleportation metaphor. The contributors increase in confidence in using the VR assembly shifted the focus towards the creative aspects of engaging with the content, especially in the workshops that took place at a later stage in the process. This is consistent with the findings of Zhang [3], who argue that during technology development, the involvement of older users is crucial, especially if the final goal is the adoption of technology. [24].

For UT, one of the most striking findings was the evolution of the preferences of the contributors as they interacted with the technology. For example, while live streaming was initially considered a priority, this changed once contributors received live-like footage (live streaming footage recorded earlier). The limitations in video quality led to a diminished preference for live streaming in favour of pre-recorded footage. Similarly, in the first workshop, real underwater sounds were thought to be crucial for immersion, but after interacting with the videos with real underwater sounds recorded by hydrophones, participants found that they did not match their expectation of a relaxing ambience. Hence, we have used an ambient underwater sound in the consequent prototypes.

Another example of this evolution occurred during the ROV trials. Initially, contributors viewed interaction with the underwater environment strictly negatively, as disruptive to the environment and in conflict with the environmental preservation motivations of the group. However, ROV's teleoperation capabilities introduced a new dimension of engagement, and contributors became enthusiastic about more direct interactivity. The session provided suggestions for features such as a robotic arm to "collect samples".

B. *Immersive experience for older adults*

A variety of immersive experiences have different levels of immersion based on the technology used to deliver them and the implementation of the experience. Immersion is an objective factor in a system that mirrors the extent to which technology can support natural sensorimotor alternatives to perception [25]. The contributing factors are typically related to the real world, mainly the hardware specifications or the design of the system, such as resolution, panoramic view, audio input and generally the number of outside physical realities that are blocked by the system [26]. The importance of this was clear from the beginning, in both packages, with members of the codesign team expressing discomfort with the headset. This is all related to the weight distribution of the headset [27] using the original strap, as it adds pressure on the forehead of the user and strain on the neck. This issue has been solved by purchasing a custom head strap that allows weight distribution, transferring the pressure from the forehead to the rest of the strap (Figure 5). Although the new strap increased the overall weight of the system, the contributors reported an improvement in wearing the VR headset, which, in turn, improved the quality of the experience. The new head strap also reduced the amount of light reaching the user's eyes through an improved light blocker that sat closer to the face.

Focusing on the digital content is paramount to immerse the player in the digital environment and gives the user a sense of presence (SoP), the sensation of leaving their current location, and they transport to a virtual environment where they act as if they are physically there, perceiving virtual objects and individuals as real [26] [28] [29]. For the HXR, in our approach to increase the SoP for our contributors, we introduce multisensory inputs using visual, audio and touch. Many of the historical artefacts are interactable, with the user having the ability to grab them from proximity or from a distance (Figure 6).

Audio textures are used for simple interactions or for impacts between swords and other objects in the environment in order to give user situational awareness [30]. These interactions are accompanied by haptic feedback in the form of small vibrations with different amplitudes and intensities in order to trigger tasks [31] and enhance the level of immersion for the user. Multisensory interaction was one of the codesign group's priorities with an initial discussion about implementing hand tracking in order to simplify the interaction metaphor versus keeping the controllers with a simplified version of the button mapping. The contributors opted for continued use of the controllers as they did not want to lose the haptic feedback.

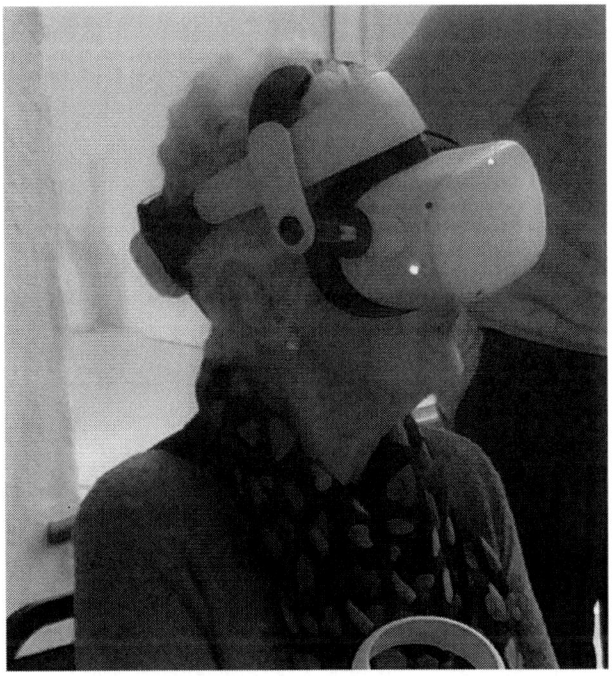

Figure 5. We replaced the original elasticated strap for the headset with a more mechanical strap that distributes the weight of the VR headset equally.

For the UT, immersion was embodied through a bimodal distribution. Many contributors expressed interest in highly stimulating and relaxing experiences, depending on the context. For example, some valued the calmness and meditative quality of simply observing marine life, while others were drawn to active gamified elements that encouraged exploration and learning. This dual demand for contrasting modes presented a design challenge, but also highlighted the potential versatility of the system by catering to diverse user needs.

The codesign exploratory approach of the ICONIC project was aimed at creating a technological base for each of the four technologies, with the intention of one or more social enterprises to take over the development and turn each prototype into a product developed by the local community for the local community. This approach meant that we did not run motion sickness tests with our codesign groups, although we encourage them at each session to report any symptoms. The only reports we had were about headset comfort and controller usability issues, with some contributors struggling to reach certain buttons or hold a controller in hand for relatively long periods of time. All reported issues were solved or mitigated, for example, we used a strap that distributes the head set weight to make it more comfortable, elasticated straps for controllers that keep the controllers attached and the implementation of all the actions on one, easy-to-reach, button.

Figure 6. The interaction works for nearby objects or for objects in the distance. The feedback is in the form of visual highlight, haptic feedback and audio for when the object lands in the user's hand.

V. Conclusion and Future Work

The findings of this study underscore the critical need for user-centred design in the development of immersive XR applications tailored for older adults. Through an iterative development process and intergenerational codesign workshops, this research has demonstrated that immersive XR technologies have substantial potential to recreate cultural heritage sites and underwater environments in ways that are engaging and meaningful for older users. However, the successful adoption of these technologies depends on addressing key design challenges that include the creation of intuitive locomotion and interaction mechanisms, simplified control schemes, and ergonomic considerations to enhance comfort and reduce physical strain. The simplified locomotion and controls gave contributors confidence in using the VR headset and as a result they shifted their focus from usability and hardware engagement to a more creative attitude, exploring various ways to engage with heritage artefacts.

Moreover, factors such as accessibility, affordability, and hardware usability emerged as essential priorities for older contributors, emphasizing the importance of reducing barriers to engagement. To address affordability, contributors chose an affordable device, although its limited technical capabilities presented a challenge in creating a rich visual environment. For usability and accessibility, we worked in partnership with the codesign team to increase comfort and accessibility to the controllers by using dedicated straps that keep the controllers attached to the hand and for the headset, we used dedicated strap that distributes the weight equally around the user's head. In addition, we designed and implemented one button that adapts to the user's actions in the virtual world, simplifies the interaction process and reduces cognitive load. These insights provide a foundation for designing inclusive and effective XR applications, not only for older adults but for broader intergenerational audiences.

Although we had a large codesign group with over 90 people recruited and 36 attendances for the combined HXR and UT work packages, we need to evaluate the developed technologies with a wider group of participants. We are currently in the process of conducting evaluation sessions with intergenerational groups of young and old adults and industry partners to evaluate the findings. The outcome of these evaluation sessions will inform the next stages of the project with one of the key elements to be explored is the development of a simplified controller focused on increased usability, personalisation and to reduce cognitive load that is aimed at older adults with limited mobility.

Future research should explore adaptive design approaches that further refine these experiences, as well as investigate strategies to improve long-term engagement and accessibility. By addressing these challenges, immersive XR applications can become powerful tools to enhance cultural engagement and expand the possibilities of virtual exploration for older adults.

Acknowledgments

This paper is presented on behalf of the ICONIC project that includes Katharine Willis, Daniel Maudlin, Chunxu Li, Sheena Asthana, Kerry Howell, Shangming Zhou, Emmanuel Ifeachor, and Hannah Bradwell as co-applicants and advisors and Lauren Tenn (Media and Administration Officer). Intergenerational co-creation of novel technologies to reconnect digitally excluded people with community & cultural landscapes in coastal economies (ICONIC) is funded by UK Research and Innovation Engineering and Physical Sciences Research Council Grant Ref: EP/W024357/1.

We thank Ocean Conservation Trust, Cotehele National Trust, Marine Station staff, Oliver Smith and Benjamin Buckfield-Richards for their contribution to this project.

References

[1] M. N. Varga and D. Bazazian, "Interactive Heritage Site Mobile Application on Artworks," in *Advances in Representation: New AI- and XR-Driven Transdisciplinarity*, A. Giordano, M. Russo, and R. Spallone, Eds., Cham: Springer Nature Switzerland, 2024, pp. 125–139, ISBN: 978-3-031-62963-1. DOI: 10.1007/978-3-031-62963-1_8.

[2] E. Ch'ng, Y. Li, S. Cai, and F.-T. Leow, "The Effects of VR Environments on the Acceptance, Experience, and Expectations of Cultural Heritage Learning," *J. Comput. Cult. Herit.*, vol. 13, no. 1, pp. 1–21, Feb. 2020, ISSN: 1556-4673. DOI: 10.1145/3352933.

[3] M. Zhang, "Older people's attitudes towards emerging technologies: A systematic literature review," *Public Understanding of Science*, vol. 32, no. 8, pp. 948–968, Nov. 2023, ISSN: 0963-6625. DOI: 10.1177/09636625231171677.

[4] K. Ijaz *et al.*, "Design Considerations for Immersive Virtual Reality Applications for Older Adults: A Scoping Review," *Multimodal Technologies and Interaction*, vol. 6, no. 7, p. 60, 7 Jul. 2022, ISSN: 2414-4088. DOI: 10.3390/mti6070060.

[5] A. V. Reyes, M. N. Varga, H. Bradwell, and R. Baxter, "Unlocking Social Innovation in XR for Healthcare in Coastal Communities," in *2023 IEEE Conference on Virtual Reality and 3D User Interfaces Abstracts and Workshops (VRW)*, Mar. 2023, pp. 128–131. DOI: 10.1109/VRW58643.2023.00032.

[6] A. Veliz Reyes *et al.*, "Codesign principles for the effective development of digital heritage extended reality systems for health interventions in rural communities," *CoDesign*, vol. 20, no. 2, pp. 295–312, Apr. 2024. ISSN: 1571-0882. DOI: 10.1080/15710882.2024.2349588.

[7] F. Gradinger, J. Elston, S. Asthana, S. Martin, and R. Byng, "Reflections on the Researcher-in-Residence model co-producing knowledge for action in an Integrated Care Organisation: A mixed methods case study using an impact survey and field notes," *Evidence & Policy*, vol. 15, no. 2, pp. 197–215, May 2019. DOI: 10.1332/174426419X15538508969850.

[8] A. C. Whittaker *et al.*, "O.1.2-10 intergenerational co-production to increase physical activity and social connectivity for health in the goald project (generating older active lives digitally)," Sep. 2023, eprint: https://academic.oup.com/eurpub/article-pdf/33/Supplement_1/ckad133.097/51496965/ckad133.097.pdf, [Online]. Available: https://doi.org/10.1093/eurpub/ckad133.097 (visited on 12/23/2024).

[9] L. Wareing, N. Dunn, and P. A. Rodgers, "Levelling up north of england for rural youth: Co-design possibilities and challenges," *Blucher Design Proceedings*, vol. 9, no. 5, pp. 506–518, 2021, ISSN: 2318-6968. DOI: http://dx.doi.org/10.5151/ead2021-157.

[10] N. Y. Agency, "Overlooked: Young people and rural youth services," National Youth Agency, Tech. Rep., 2021, pp. 1–20.

[11] G. O. for Science, "Mental capital and wellbeing: Making the most of ourselves in the 21st century," UK Government Office for Science, Oct. 22, 2018.

[12] R. Jones *et al.*, "Addressing Digital Exclusion via the Inter-Generational Codesign of Extended Reality, Underwater Telepresence, Social Games, and Voice AI Technologies," *International Journal On Advances in Intelligent Systems*, vol. 17, no. 3&4, Nov. 2024, ISSN: 1942-2679.

[13] J. Grellier *et al.*, "BlueHealth: A study programme protocol for mapping and quantifying the potential benefits to public health and well-being from Europe's blue spaces," *BMJ open*, vol. 7, no. 6, e016188, Jun. 2017, ISSN: 2044-6055. DOI: 10.1136/bmjopen-2017-016188.

[14] T. B. Sheridan, "Musings on Telepresence and Virtual Presence," *Presence: Teleoperators and Virtual Environments*, vol. 1, no. 1, pp. 120–126, Feb. 1992. DOI: 10.1162/pres.1992.1.1.120.

[15] O. Hagen, A. Aly, R. Jones, M. Varga, and D. Bazazian, "Beyond the surface: A scoping review of vision-based underwater experience technologies and user studies," *Intelligent Marine Technology and Systems*, vol. 2, no. 1, p. 19, Jun. 2024, ISSN: 2948-1953. DOI: 10.1007/s44295-024-00034-3.

[16] C. Macklin and J. Sharp, *Games, design and play : a detailed approach to iterative game design / Colleen Macklin, John Sharp.* eng, First edition. Boston, MA ; Addison-Wesley, 2016, ISBN: 0134392078.

[17] "Meta Quest 3," [Online]. Available: https://www.meta.com/gb/quest/quest-3/ (visited on 03/01/2025).

[18] "Meta," Meta, [Online]. Available: https://www.meta.com/ (visited on 03/01/2025).

[19] F. Remondino, "Heritage Recording and 3D Modeling with Photogrammetry and 3D Scanning," *Remote Sensing*, vol. 3, no. 6, pp. 1104–1138, Jun. 2011, ISSN: 2072-4292. DOI: 10.3390/rs3061104.

[20] "Fab," Fab.com, 2025, [Online]. Available: https://www.fab.com/ (visited on 03/01/2025).

[21] "Unreal Engine," Unreal Engine, 2025, [Online]. Available: https://www.unrealengine.com/en-US/home (visited on 03/01/2025).

[22] Z. Wu *et al.*, "Toward Making Virtual Reality (VR) More Inclusive for Older Adults: Investigating Aging Effect on Target Selection and Manipulation Tasks in VR," in *Proceedings of the 2024 CHI Conference on Human Factors in Computing Systems*, ser. CHI '24, New York, NY, USA: Association for Computing Machinery, May 11, 2024, pp. 1–17, ISBN: 9798400703300. DOI: 10.1145/3613904.3642558.

[23] S. Baker *et al.*, "Interrogating Social Virtual Reality as a Communication Medium for Older Adults," *Proc. ACM Hum.-Comput. Interact.*, vol. 3, 149:1–149:24, CSCW Nov. 7, 2019. DOI: 10.1145/3359251.

[24] E. Vaportzis, M. Giatsi Clausen, and A. J. Gow, "Older Adults Perceptions of Technology and Barriers to Interacting with Tablet Computers: A Focus Group Study," *Frontiers in Psychology*, vol. 8, p. 1687, Oct. 2017, ISSN: 1664-1078. DOI: 10.3389/fpsyg.2017.01687.

[25] M. Slater, "Immersion and the illusion of presence in virtual reality," *British Journal of Psychology*, vol. 109, no. 3, pp. 431–433, Aug. 2018, ISSN: 0007-1269, 2044-8295. DOI: 10.1111/bjop.12305.

[26] J.-C. Servotte *et al.*, "Virtual Reality Experience: Immersion, Sense of Presence, and Cybersickness," *Clinical Simulation in Nursing*, vol. 38, pp. 35–43, Jan. 2020, ISSN: 1876-1399. DOI: 10.1016/j.ecns.2019.09.006.

[27] J. R. Bruun-Pedersen, S. Serafin, and L. B. Kofoed, "Going Outside While Staying Inside — Exercise Motivation with Immersive vs. Non–immersive Recreational Virtual Environment Augmentation for Older Adult Nursing Home Residents," in *2016 IEEE International Conference on Healthcare Informatics (ICHI)*, Oct. 2016, pp. 216–226. DOI: 10.1109/ICHI.2016.31.

[28] M. Slater, "Measuring Presence: A Response to the Witmer and Singer Presence Questionnaire," *Presence*, vol. 8, no. 5, pp. 560–565, Oct. 1999, ISSN: 1054-7460. DOI: 10.1162/105474699566477.

[29] M. Slater and M. V. Sanchez-Vives, "Enhancing Our Lives with Immersive Virtual Reality," *Frontiers in Robotics and AI*, vol. 3, Dec. 2016, ISSN: 2296-9144. DOI: 10.3389/frobt.2016.00074.

[30] Y.-C. Yang, "Role-play in Virtual Reality Game for the Senior," in *Proceedings of the 2019 7th International Conference on Information and Education Technology*, ser. ICIET 2019, New York, NY, USA: Association for Computing Machinery, Mar. 29, 2019, pp. 31–35, ISBN: 978-1-4503-6639-7. DOI: 10.1145/3323771.3323812.

[31] É. Ouellet, B. Boller, N. Corriveau-Lecavalier, S. Cloutier, and S. Belleville, "The Virtual Shop: A new immersive virtual reality environment and scenario for the assessment of everyday memory," *Journal of Neuroscience Methods*, vol. 303, pp. 126–135, Jun. 1, 2018, ISSN: 1872-678X. DOI: 10.1016/j.jneumeth.2018.03.010. pmid: 29581009.

Addressing the Symbol Grounding Problem in VR

Muneo Kitajima
Nagaoka University of Technology
Nagaoka, Niigata, Japan
Email: mkitajima@kjs.nagaokaut.ac.jp

Makoto Toyota
T-Method
Chiba, Japan
Email: pubmtoyota@mac.com

Katsuko T. Nakahira
Nagaoka University of Technology
Nagaoka, Niigata, Japan
Email: katsuko@vos.nagaokaut.ac.jp

***Abstract*— A Virtual Reality (VR) environment presents objects that the user perceives and interacts with. It then transitions to the next state, reflecting the content of the interaction that has occurred as a result of the user's perception of the objects. For the interaction between the VR environment and the user to continue seamlessly, the meanings assigned to the objects in the VR environment by the creator of VR applications and the meanings held by the user experiencing them must be consistent. In this study, we propose a method to realize seamless interaction between VR environments and users by considering the objects presented by VR environments as symbols and capturing the relationship between the meanings they contain and the meanings held by the users who experience them through the symbol grounding problem, which is regarded as a challenging issue in the field of artificial intelligence. Based on the Mode Human Processor with Realtime Constraints (MHP/RT), which is a cognitive architecture that can deal with action selections in everyday environments, we focus on the fact that the content of human action selections is based on memes that are handed down from generation to generation and should provide a basis for his/her understanding of the situation of the surrounding world, and suggest that the symbol grounding problem can be solved by observing and identifying memes.**

Keywords*— *The Symbol Grounding Problem; Meme; Virtual Reality; Artificial Intelligence; MHP/RT; Structured Meme Theory.

I. Introduction

Humans acquire information about the outside world through the five senses, and select and execute appropriate actions for the situation at hand by operating the Perceptual, Cognitive, and Motor (PCM) processes. Perceived information is encoded and represented as symbols in the perceptual process, which makes it possible to think in the cognitive process. In the thinking process, memory is used to successively transform the symbols into new representations. Part of the result of thinking gives a representation of a sequence of actions that can be performed in the motor process. Based on the idea that human intelligence can be captured by thought processes that manipulate symbols, Newell proposed the Physical Symbol System as a theory of human intelligence [1]. This idea provided the foundation for Soar [2][3], which is one of the successful cognitive architectures.

The information that is input to the perceptual process through the sensory organs has its source in the real world. According to the sequence of actions represented by symbols generated through the PCM processes, actions are performed in the real world and the real world is updated. When we try to artificially realize such interactions that humans perform in the real world using a physical symbol system, the system must have the ability to link the symbolic representations to the references in the real world and to acquire meaningful understanding from interactions with the environment.

The realization of this capability is a fundamental challenge in Artificial Intelligence (AI) research and is referred to as the Symbol Grounding Problem (SGP) [4]. It concerns the ability of a machine to connect its symbolic representations to real-world references and acquire meaningful understanding from its interaction with its environment. In other words, it is about how machines can understand and represent the meaning of objects, concepts, and events in the world. Without the ability to ground symbolic representations in the real world, machines cannot acquire the rich and complex meanings needed for intelligent behavior such as language processing, image recognition, and decision making. Addressing the SGP is crucial to building machines that can perceive, reason, and act like humans.

One of the environments in which humans interact is a Virtual Reality (VR) environment. In a VR environment, users can interact with artificial 3D visual environments or environments involving other sensory modalities using computer modeling and simulation. VR applications immerse the users in a computer-generated environment that simulates reality. In a VR environment, user interaction proceeds through user-perceivable objects provided by VR applications. The meaning that the user gives to the objects generated by the VR applications determines how the user interacts with the objects. The VR applications can achieve a seamless interaction by having the ability to appropriately handle the meanings given by the user to the objects. Here, it can be seen that the SGP is not unrelated to the realization of seamless VR environments. In this paper, we propose a method to deal with the SGP in VR.

This paper is organized as follows. Section II presents the framework for dealing with interaction via objects. Section III describes the interaction between self and an object, how to capture the SGP in AI from the interaction perspective, and how to capture the interaction between self and VR. Section IV suggests how to generate VR environments that could guarantee symbol grounding.

II. Interaction via Objects

In this section, the aspects of individual human interaction through objects are classified in Section II-A and the perceptual, cognitive, and motor processes and memories of each human who interacts with the object are described in Section II-B.

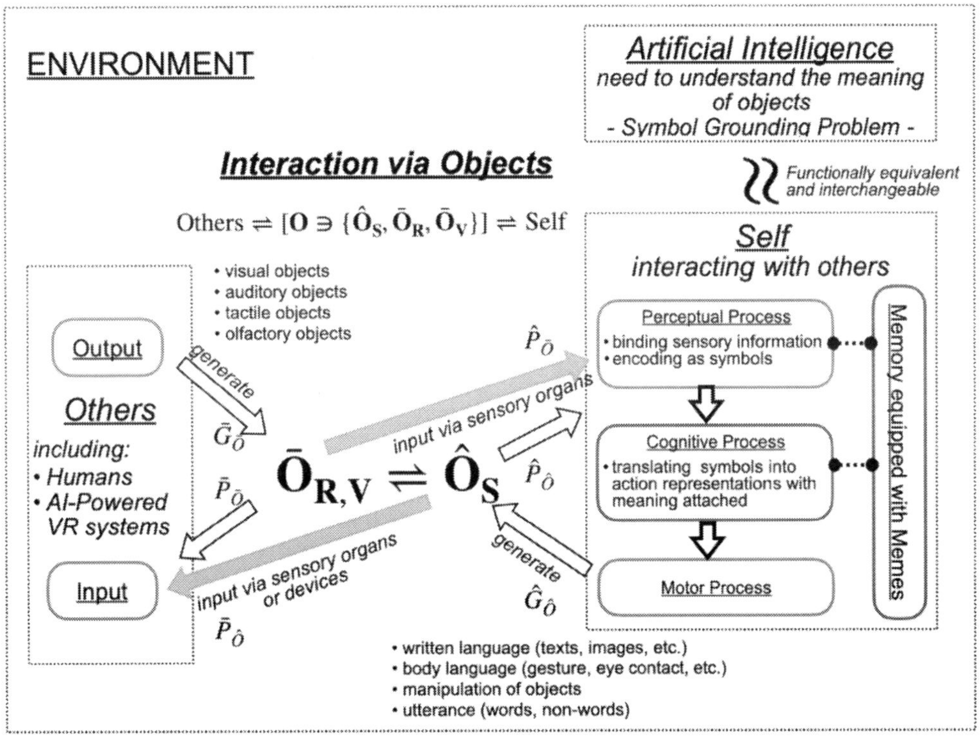

Figure 1. Interaction via objects

A. Interaction Types

Individuals live their daily lives interacting with a large number of objects that exist around them. Objects are classified according to whether they are directly or indirectly interacted with by self and by whom they are created. There are three types of objects defined as follows:

- $\hat{\mathbf{O}}_\mathbf{S}$: Real objects that are directly generated by self, e.g., utterance, written text, drawings, gestures, modeling, etc.
- $\bar{\mathbf{O}}_\mathbf{R}$: Real objects generated by other human beings with whom self is directly interacting.
- $\bar{\mathbf{O}}_\mathbf{V}$: Objects generated by a machine or other human beings with whom self is not directly interacting.

These three types of objects are collectively represented as $\mathbf{O}$ ($\ni \{\hat{\mathbf{O}}_\mathbf{S}, \bar{\mathbf{O}}_\mathbf{R}, \bar{\mathbf{O}}_\mathbf{V}\}$). In Figure 1, $\mathbf{O}$ is placed in the center, "Self" interacting with $\mathbf{O}$ on its right side, and "Others" interacting with $\mathbf{O}$ on its left side. On top of "Self" is an "Artificial Intelligence" that is functionally equivalent to self and can be replaced. Self operates the PCM processes to generate the objects $\hat{\mathbf{O}}_\mathbf{S}$ ($\hat{G}_{\hat{O}}$). Self also perceives them ($\hat{P}_{\hat{O}}$). The objects self perceives include the objects $\bar{\mathbf{O}}_{\mathbf{R},\mathbf{V}}$ generated by others ($\hat{P}_{\bar{O}}$). Meanwhile, others generate the objects $\bar{\mathbf{O}}_{\mathbf{R},\mathbf{V}}$ ($\bar{G}_{\bar{O}}$). If the other is a human being, it runs the PCM process, which is equivalent to the one self runs, to generate the objects $\bar{\mathbf{O}}_\mathbf{R}$ ($\bar{G}_{\bar{O}_R}$). Machines run their own generative mechanisms to produce the objects $\bar{\mathbf{O}}_\mathbf{V}$ as output ($\bar{G}_{\bar{O}_V}$). The input to the others are the objects $\bar{\mathbf{O}}_{\mathbf{R},\mathbf{V}}$ generated by the others themselves ($\bar{P}_{\bar{O}}$), or the objects $\hat{\mathbf{O}}_\mathbf{S}$ generated by self ($\bar{P}_{\hat{O}}$). In summary, interaction via objects can be expressed as follows:

$$\text{Others} \rightleftharpoons [\mathbf{O} \ni \{\hat{\mathbf{O}}_\mathbf{S}, \bar{\mathbf{O}}_\mathbf{R}, \bar{\mathbf{O}}_\mathbf{V}\}] \rightleftharpoons \text{Self}$$

B. Interaction between Self and O

The interaction between self and $\mathbf{O}$ is performed by the PCM processes that the self runs, and by the memory processes that are used by the PCM processes and updated as a result of the execution of the PCM processes. This section provides an overview of the PCM and memory processes based on the Model Human Processor with Real-Time Constraints (MHP/RT), a cognitive architecture that can simulate everyday action selections [5][6][7].

1) The PCM Process: When interacting with objects in the environment, humans respond to physical and chemical stimuli emitted from the objects by sensory nerves located at the interface with the environment and take in environmental information in the body. Figure 2, adapted from [8, Figure 1] with modification, shows the PCM process, based on the MHP/RT cognitive architecture [6][7], by which environmental information is taken into the body via sensory nerves, processed in the brain, and then acted upon by the external world via motor nerves. This process uses memory, which is modeled as the Multi-Dimensional Memory Frame. It consists of the Perceptual-, Behavior-, Motor-, Relation-, and Word-Multi-Dimensional Memory Frame. The Perceptual-Multi-Dimensional Memory Frame overlaps with the Behavior-, Relation-, and Word-Multi-Dimensional Memory Frame. This

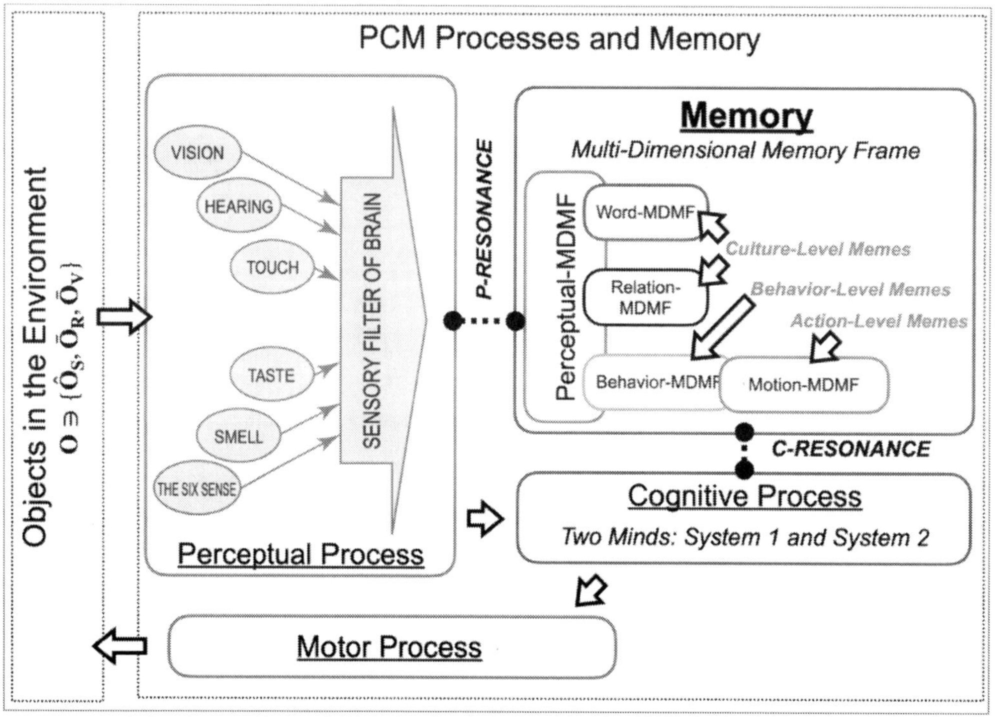

Figure 2. PCM process and memory

is the unique and indispensable configuration of memories defined by the Multi-Dimensional Memory Frame for spreading activation from the Perceptual- to Motor-Multi-Dimensional Memory Frame, which connects perception with bodily movements.

Perceptual information taken in from the environment through sensory organs *resonates* with information in the Multi-Dimensional Memory Frame, which is called P-Resonance. In Figure 2, this process is indicated by the symbol •—•. Resonance occurs first in the Perceptual-Multi-Dimensional Memory Frame and activates the memory network. After that, the activation spreads to the memory networks that overlap the Perceptual-Multi-Dimensional Memory Frame, and finally to the Motor-Multi-Dimensional Memory Frame. In cognitive processing by Two Minds [9][10], conscious processing by System 2, which utilizes the Word- and Relation-Multi-Dimensional Memory Frame via C-Resonance, and unconscious processing by System 1, which utilizes the Behavior- and Motor-Multi-Dimensional Memory Frame via C-Resonance, proceed in an interrelated manner. The motor sequences are expressed according to the Motor-Multi-Dimensional Memory Frame. The memories involved in the production of actions are updated to reflect the traces of their use process and influence the future action selection process.

2) Memory and Memes: When the PCM process is running, the contents of Perceptual-Multi-Dimensional Memory Frame are updated in response to the perceptual process, those of Word-, Relation-, and Behavior-Multi-Dimensional Memory Frame are updated in response to the cognitive process, and those of Motor-Multi-Dimensional Memory Frame are updated in response to the motor process. Alternatively, the memory system can be viewed from the perspective of memory use. The integrated sensory information first activates the Perceptual-Multi-Dimensional Memory Frame; then the activation spreads to the Word-, Relation-, and Behavior-Multi-Dimensional Memory Frame, and finally to the Motor-Multi-Dimensional Memory Frame bound to the motor nerves. The basis of behavior is *imitation*; do as what you see. Therefore, behaviors that can be imitated across generations are preserved as sustainable behaviors. In this way, we can organize the Multi-Dimensional Memory Frame, which is used by the PCM processes and updated by their execution, in terms of *memes* that can be inherited across generations [11].

Word is considered the archetype of meme [12]. Words, i.e., symbols, are gradually incorporated into the environment in the form of *thesauruses*, i.e., lists of words in groups of synonyms and related concepts; followed by incorporation of languages used for person-to-person communication, *individual languages*, which might include not only direct but also metaphorical uses; and lastly incorporated are languages used in cultural contexts, *cultural languages*, in which appropriate understanding of common sense that has been established in the specific community, is essential for successful communication. These three forms circulate among people and persist from generation to generation [13].

Thesauruses, individual languages, and cultural languages increase their complexity in this order in terms of the patterns they are linked with the objects in the environment. The-

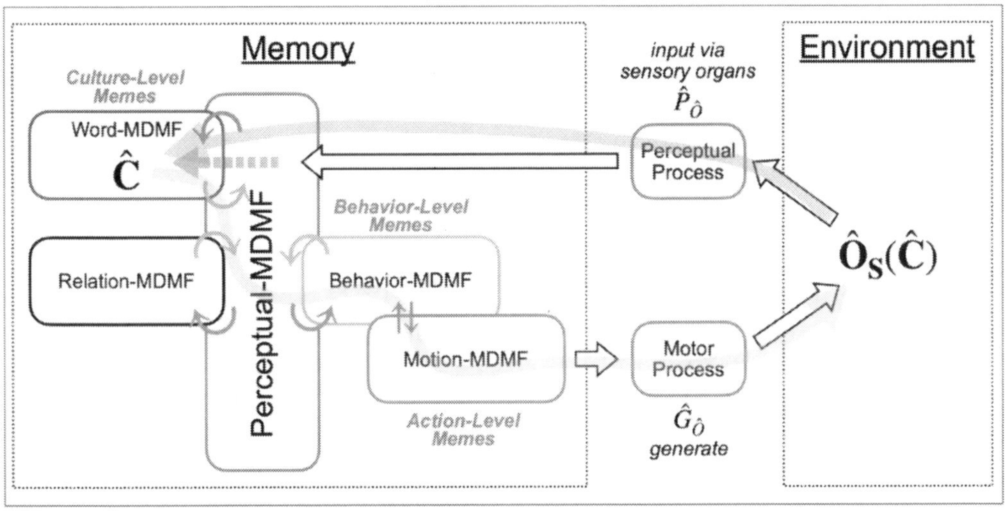

Figure 3. Symbol grounding when the self generates an object $\hat{\mathbf{O}}_{\mathbf{S}}(\hat{\mathbf{C}})$ that embodies the concept $\hat{\mathbf{C}}$

sauruses are associated with the objects in the environment that are encoded in the neural networks in the initial development stage from the birth to 3 years. Individual languages are associated with not only the objects in the environment but also the symbols that have already been incorporated in the environment. The same is true for cultural languages. In the Structured Meme Theory (SMT) [11], which is the memory construct to be used and updated by the MHP/RT, the patterns that represent the thesauruses, individual languages, and cultural languages are called action-level meme (A-meme), behavior-level meme (B-meme), and culture-level meme (C-meme), respectively.

As shown in the rounded corner rectangle "Memory" in Figure 2, the relationships between the three levels of memes and the Multi-Dimensional Memory Frame are as follows:

- A-memes represent bodily actions stored in the Motor-Multi-Dimensional Memory Frame.
- B-memes represent behaviors in the environment stored in the Behavior-Multi-Dimensional Memory Frame.
- C-memes represent culture stored in the Relation- and Word-Multi-Dimensional Memory Frame.

III. Details of Interaction between Self and O

This section describes how individual human perceptual, cognitive, and motor processes and memory work for each of the interaction types introduced in Section II, and clarifies how the symbolic grounding problem is involved and solved.

A. *Interaction between Self and* $\hat{\mathbf{O}}_{\mathbf{S}}$

The process of generating an object $\hat{\mathbf{O}}_{\mathbf{S}}(\hat{\mathbf{C}})$ that represents the concept $\hat{\mathbf{C}}$ by self ($\hat{G}_{\hat{O}(\hat{C})}$) and perceiving the generated result ($\hat{P}_{\hat{O}(\hat{C})}$) is shown in Figure 3 using Figure 2 as a basis. According to this process, an object that matches the concept is generated. Figure 4 shows the flow of activation within the Multi-Dimensional Memory Frame involved in this process.

1) The concept $\hat{\mathbf{C}}$ is represented as a symbol within C-memes, and the nodes associated with it in the Word-Multi-Dimensional Memory Frame are activated.
2) Activation spreads from the Word- to Perceptual-Multi-Dimensional Memory Frame.
3) Activation spreads from the Perceptual- to Relation-Multi-Dimensional Memory Frame that encodes C-memes, and reaches Motor-Multi-Dimensional Memory Frame encoding A-memes via Behavior-Multi-Dimensional Memory Frame encoding B-memes.
4) According to the contents of activated Motor-Multi-Dimensional Memory Frame, the motor process operates to express bodily movements, which result in the generation of object $\hat{\mathbf{O}}_{\mathbf{S}}(\hat{\mathbf{C}})$ in the environment.

Figure 4. Object Generation Process

This object generation process is indicated along the thick orange arrow in Figure 3. It is denoted symbolically as follows:

Generation Path [G-SS]

$$\hat{\mathbf{C}} \Rightarrow \left[\frac{\text{W-, R-, B-MDMF} \rightleftharpoons \text{M-MDMF}}{\text{P-MDMF}}\right] \Rightarrow \hat{\mathbf{O}}_{\mathbf{S}}(\hat{\mathbf{C}}) \tag{1}$$

Here, the part indicated by $[\;\cdots\;]$ in the middle of the expression shows the process of spreading activation in the Multi-Dimensional Memory Frame from the viewpoint of the activated location in the memory. The symbol [G-SS] reads as follows; [**G**enerate - symbol in **S**elf via memory of **S**elf].

The generation process [G-SS] can be rearranged from the perspective of memes, i.e., memories of contents, as follows:

Meme-Mapping

$$\hat{\mathbf{C}} \Rightarrow \left[\frac{\text{C-memes} \rightleftharpoons \text{B-memes}}{\text{P-MDMF}} \rightleftharpoons \text{A-memes}\right]_{\text{M-S}} \Rightarrow \hat{\mathbf{O}}_{\mathbf{S}}(\hat{\mathbf{C}}) \tag{2}$$

The generated object $\hat{\mathbf{O}}_{\mathbf{S}}(\hat{\mathbf{C}})$ shown on the right end is associated with a state in which the C-, B-, and A-memes activated in the process of spreading activation in the Multi-Dimensional Memory Frame starting from the concept $\hat{\mathbf{C}}$ shown on the left end. The association is represented in the middle, $[\cdots]_{\text{M-S}}$, called "meme-mapping" from $\hat{\mathbf{C}}$ to $\hat{\mathbf{O}}_{\mathbf{S}}(\hat{\mathbf{C}})$.

1) Perceive $\hat{\mathbf{O}}_{\mathbf{S}}(\hat{\mathbf{C}})$ and the activation spreads within the Perceptual-Multi-Dimensional Memory Frame.
2) The activation spread from the Perceptual- to Word-Multi-Dimensional Memory Frame results in the activation of symbol related to the perceptual representation.

Figure 5. Object Recognition Process

Figure 5 shows the object recognition process. The thick blue arrow in Figure 3 indicates this process. [R-SS] reads [**R**ecognize object - generated by **S**elf using memory of **S**elf].

Recognition Path [R-SS]

$$\hat{\mathbf{O}}_{\mathbf{S}}(\hat{\mathbf{C}}) \Rightarrow \left[\frac{\text{P-MDFM}}{\text{W-MDMF}}\right] \Rightarrow \hat{\mathbf{C}} \tag{3}$$

In [R-SS], if the concept $\hat{\mathbf{C}}$ is strongly activated, then $\hat{\mathbf{O}}_{\mathbf{S}}(\hat{\mathbf{C}})$ correctly realizes $\hat{\mathbf{C}}$ in the real world. In this case, [G-SS] and [R-SS] are connected and closed, and the symbol $\hat{\mathbf{C}}$ and $\hat{\mathbf{O}}_{\mathbf{S}}(\hat{\mathbf{C}})$ are cognitively replaceable, which is represented by $\hat{\mathbf{C}} \equiv \hat{\mathbf{O}}_{\mathbf{S}}(\hat{\mathbf{C}})$. This state can be regarded as a state in which symbol grounding has been achieved within self (see Figure 6).

- Symbol $\mathbf{C}$ in C-memes activates B- and A-memes via the Perceptual-Multi-Dimensional Memory Frame to generate $\hat{\mathbf{O}}_{\mathbf{S}}(\mathbf{C})$.
- Perception of $\hat{\mathbf{O}}_{\mathbf{S}}(\mathbf{C})$ activates $\mathbf{C}$ and its associated activation pattern in the Multi-Dimensional Memory Frame.
- The perceptual representation of $\hat{\mathbf{O}}_{\mathbf{S}}(\mathbf{C})$ in the Perceptual-Multi-Dimensional Memory Frame is associated with $\mathbf{C}$ in Word-Multi-Dimensional Memory Frame.
- In the future, $\mathbf{C}$ in the Word-Multi-Dimensional Memory Frame activates perceptual representation of $\hat{\mathbf{O}}_{\mathbf{S}}(\mathbf{C})$ even if it does not exist in the real world, which enables the self to perceptually simulate the concept along with the activation of the Multi-Dimensional Memory Frame necessary to actually generate the object.

Figure 6. Symbol Grounding of Concept $\mathbf{C}$ in Self

B. *The Symbol Grounding Problem in AI*

The symbol grounding problem in AI shown in Figure 1 is solved by the fact that an activation pattern equivalent to the activation pattern of memes in the Multi-Dimensional Memory Frame that occurs in the process of generating self's $\hat{\mathbf{O}}_{\mathbf{S}}$ also occurs in AI. By ensuring that the meme-mappings occur within AI and self are equivalent, i.e., $[\cdots]_{\text{M-AI}} \equiv [\cdots]_{\text{M-S}}$, AI can be a substitute for self. This is summarized in Figure 7, where "Perceptual-Information-Encoding-in-AI" is the substitute for the Perceptual-Multi-Dimensional Memory Frame of human to perform A/D transformation to input the real world data to the AI system. Since the memes are knowledge passed down from generation to generation, it is considered possible to represent them by symbols. The Perceptual-Information-Encoding-in-AI can also be represented in symbols by encoding environmental information by sensors that perform the same function as sensory organs. The symbol grounding problem in AI is thought to be solved by elucidating memes.

1) The symbol $\hat{\mathbf{C}}$, which is common to self's, in C-memes activates the Perceptual-Information-Encoding-in-AI as well as the associated C-memes in AI.
2) B-memes are activated via the activated portion of Perceptual-Information-Encoding-in-AI.
3) The part of A-memes that overlap the activated B-memes is activated.

The steps 1, 2, and 3 constitute the meme-mapping of AI.

4) What is expressed by the activated A-memes is implemented in the real world via appropriate actuators.
5) Upon input of the object $\hat{\mathbf{O}}_{\mathbf{S}}(\hat{\mathbf{C}})$ in AI, activation spreads in the Perceptual-Information-Encoding-in-AI, followed by the activation of the symbol $\hat{\mathbf{C}}$ in C-memes.
6) The part in the Perceptual-Information-Encoding-in-AI that corresponds to $\hat{\mathbf{O}}_{\mathbf{S}}(\hat{\mathbf{C}})$ and the symbol $\hat{\mathbf{C}}$ integrate the C-, B-, and A-memes activated in the steps 1, 2, and 3 to form an integrated association. At this point, $\hat{\mathbf{C}} \equiv \hat{\mathbf{O}}_{\mathbf{S}}(\hat{\mathbf{C}})$ is established by AI by means of $[\cdots]_{\text{M-AI}}$, in other words, the symbol $\hat{\mathbf{C}}$ both the AI and the self commonly recognize has been grounded, secured by the relationship $[\cdots]_{\text{M-AI}} \equiv [\cdots]_{\text{M-S}}$.

Figure 7. Symbol Grounding of Concept $\hat{\mathbf{C}}$ in AI

C. *Interaction between Self and $\bar{\mathbf{O}}_{\mathbf{R}}$*

Consider the case where the other human generates an object. The object generation process for the concept $\bar{\mathbf{C}}$ performed by the other human is represented as $\bar{\mathbf{C}} \Rightarrow [\cdots] \Rightarrow \bar{\mathbf{O}}_{\mathbf{R}}(\bar{\mathbf{C}})$, which is a the-other-human's version of [G-SS]. The other human spreads activation in his/her own Multi-Dimensional Memory Frame. The meme-mapping used for the other human is denoted as $[\cdots]_{\text{M-O}}$. The self interacting with the other human who has just generated $\bar{\mathbf{O}}_{\mathbf{R}}(\bar{\mathbf{C}})$ recognizes it according to the following path:

Recognition Path for the Object Generated by Other [R-OS]

$$\bar{\mathbf{O}}_{\mathbf{R}}(\bar{\mathbf{C}}) \Rightarrow \left[\frac{\text{P-MDFM}}{\text{W-MDMF}}\right] \Rightarrow \hat{\mathbf{C}} \tag{4}$$

If the symbol $\bar{\mathbf{C}}$ ($\equiv \bar{\mathbf{O}}_{\mathbf{R}}(\bar{\mathbf{C}})$) held by the other human and the symbol $\hat{\mathbf{C}}$ held by the self are identical, the symbol is transmitted through the object expressed by the other. For example, the other person holds a certain word $\bar{\mathbf{C}}$ in his/her mind and expresses it physically through gestures, and then the self sees it and assigns the word $\hat{\mathbf{C}}$ to it. The latent word of the other is connected to the self's latent word through the physical actions of the other person. Consider the case of communication via words, where the self and the other look at a sequence of words $\tilde{\mathbf{C}}$. The self and the other perform symbol grounding according to their respective generation paths; $[\ \cdots\ ]_{\text{M-S}}$ and $[\ \cdots\ ]_{\text{M-O}}$ are included in each symbol grounding process. If the self and the other have grown up in the same environment, which is the necessary condition for them to have a common set of memes, then the relation $[\cdots]_{\text{M-S}} \equiv [\cdots]_{\text{M-O}}$ would hold, and the shared symbols have the same meaning. However, in the case of $[\ \cdots\ ]_{\text{M-S}} \neq [\ \cdots\ ]_{\text{M-O}}$, the meaning of all visually shared symbols may not be shared. For example, the phrase "see you on the ground floor" may trigger different behaviors depending on the culture to which the reader of the phrase belongs.

D. *Interaction between Self and* $\bar{\mathbf{O}}_{\mathrm{V}}$

In the case of interaction between self and other humans, the interaction is symmetric because both parties are humans. That is, in the part indicated by $[\cdots]$ that connects the symbol and the object in the generation and recognition paths, the activation spreads inside the Multi-Dimensional Memory Frame owned by self and others, respectively. On the other hand, in the case of Self–VR interaction, the generation and recognition paths on the system side are different from those on the human side. In the generation path, symbols defined in the system are converted into objects that can be perceived by the user. In the recognition path, human-generated objects are input to the system via sensors and converted into symbols that the system can handle. Both conversions are performed by programs implemented in the system.

In a VR environment, the system takes in the information emitted by human users and then determines the response to it. In any case, the input is represented as a symbol $\tilde{\mathbf{C}}$. Within the system, after setting a symbol $\bar{\bar{\mathbf{C}}}$ to be transmitted in the next cycle of interaction, the symbol-object transformation is performed and the object $\bar{\bar{\mathbf{O}}}_{\mathrm{V}}(\bar{\bar{\mathbf{C}}})$ is output to be perceived by the user. This generation path is denoted as [G-VV].

The user perceives the object $\bar{\bar{\mathbf{O}}}_{\mathrm{V}}(\bar{\bar{\mathbf{C}}})$ and recognizes it as a symbol along the recognition path [R-VS]. Let $\hat{\mathbf{C}}'$ be the recognized symbol. The user activates his/her Multi-Dimensional Memory Frame along the generation path [G-SS] for $\hat{\mathbf{C}}'$ and obtains the corresponding object $\hat{\mathbf{O}}_{\mathbf{S}}(\hat{\mathbf{C}}')$. If the relation $\hat{\mathbf{O}}_{\mathbf{S}}(\hat{\mathbf{C}}') \equiv$ (or $\approx$) $\bar{\bar{\mathbf{O}}}_{\mathrm{V}}(\bar{\bar{\mathbf{C}}})$ holds, the interaction will proceed smoothly. If not, it will fail.

IV. Method of $\bar{\mathbf{O}}_{\mathbf{V}}$ Generation with Symbol Grounding Secured

Only if the object generation path [G-VV] in the system is executed according to the user's meme mapping $[\cdots]_{\text{M-S}}$, i.e., if the meme mapping in the system is based on $[\cdots]_{\text{M-AI}}$, it is possible to proceed with an interaction that guarantees symbol grounding. Since memes are knowledge that are passed down from generation to generation, they can be represented by symbols. In this section, we add explanations for memes and suggest a method for externalizing them.

A. *Getting Memes into the Brain*

1) Action-Level Memes: During the period from birth to two to three years of age, humans generate a large number of synapses that connect neural circuits in the brain and take in as much information as possible. The rate of synapse generation is then reduced, and the distribution of information up to that point is used to determine the basic characteristics of the sensory organs. At the same time, by initiating body movements and imitating the movements of the people around them, they acquire body movements that have been formed empirically and accumulatively as individual ecology. This is formed through life's skillful method of adjusting the growth of muscles and other parts of the body to external constraints. At the same time, information from the sensory organs is linked to bodily actions. The most important bodily functions formed at this stage are the voice and hand functions.

2) Behavior-Level Memes: Later, the voice paves the way to speech; the hands pave the way to tool use. Through continuous imitation, humans learn to use the words and tools of those around them. At this time, humans acquire a new hierarchy of actions by organizing and summarizing the fact that a particular collection of sounds evokes a particular response, and that the feel of a hand experienced through tactile sensation and the movement of a tool perceived visually are captured as an unified whole via the tool. This is made possible by linking the A-memes formed on the brain circuit according to the situation in which they are used, and making them available as a coherent whole.

3) Culture-Level Memes: Furthermore, words pave the way to language, and tools pave the way to the use of more complex machines. At this stage, humans learn to act as members of the culture and civilization of the group to which they belong, not only through imitation but also through the experience of autonomous activities as members of the group. At this time, the B-level memes is extended to be used in a complex manner, and culture-specific behavior patterns are formed.

B. *Mapping Memes into Information Systems*

The mechanism by which the memes inherit information is analogous to an information system. A-memes serve as the operating system that defines general patterns of spatial-temporal behavioral functions. B-memes represent middleware that extends the general patterns to concrete patterns. C-memes act as application tools that extend the concrete patterns to the ones that work in a number of groups of people. By viewing memes as information systems, it is possible to represent human activities in various situations with symbols by observing them. Meme extraction has been attempted in some studies; the extraction of memes by observing the behavior of people trying to reach their destinations while acquiring information from information displays at railroad stations [5]; the inheritance of skills by ceramic artists through the acquisition of memes [14]; the memes used by skilled piano players during practice for a concert [15]. It is expected that memes in interaction in VR environments can also be elucidated based on these methods with appropriate modifications.

V. Conclusion

We argued that symbol grounding is realized when we perceive and recognize an object generated from a certain symbol and match it with that symbol. In the object generation process, A-, B-, and C-memes, are involved in the conversion from symbols to objects. Since memes are passed down from generation to generation, we suggested that they could be extracted by observation, referring to the previous studies [5][14][15]. These are based on the MHP/RT [5][6][7] and the SMT [11][13]. The ability to evaluate objects that are presented when users interact with VR environments from the symbol grounding perspective is an important issue in the development of seamless VR environments.

ACKNOWLEDGMENT

This work was supported by JSPS KAKENHI Grant Number 19K12246 / 19K12232 / 20H04290 / 22K12284 / 23K11334 , and National University Management Reform Promotion Project.

REFERENCES

[1] A. Newell, "Physical Symbol Systems," Cognitive Science, vol. 4, no. 2, 1980, pp. 135–183.

[2] A. Newell, Unified Theories of Cognition (The William James Lectures, 1987). Cambridge, MA: Harvard University Press, 1990.

[3] J. E. Laird, A. Newell, and P. S. Rosenbloom, "Soar: An architecture for general intelligence," Artificial Intelligence, vol. 33, 1987, pp. 1–64.

[4] "The symbol grounding problem," Physica D: Nonlinear Phenomena, vol. 42, no. 1, 1990, pp. 335–346, [retrieved: 2, 2025].

[5] M. Kitajima and M. Toyota, "Simulating navigation behaviour based on the architecture model Model Human Processor with Real-Time Constraints (MHP/RT)," Behaviour & Information Technology, vol. 31, no. 1, 2012, pp. 41–58.

[6] M. Kitajima and M. Toyota, "Decision-making and action selection in Two Minds: An analysis based on Model Human Processor with Realtime Constraints (MHP/RT)," Biologically Inspired Cognitive Architectures, vol. 5, 2013, pp. 82–93.

[7] M. Kitajima, Memory and Action Selection in Human-Machine Interaction. Wiley-ISTE, 2016.

[8] M. Kitajima et al., "Basic Senses and Their Implications for Immersive Virtual Reality Design," in AIVR 2024 : The First International Conference on Artificial Intelligence and Immersive Virtual Reality, 2024, pp. 31–38.

[9] D. Kahneman, "A Perspective on Judgment and Choice," American Psychologist, vol. 58, no. 9, 2003, pp. 697–720.

[10] D. Kahneman, Thinking, Fast and Slow. New York, NY: Farrar, Straus and Giroux, 2011.

[11] M. Toyota, M. Kitajima, and H. Shimada, "Structured Meme Theory: How is informational inheritance maintained?" in Proceedings of the 30th Annual Conference of the Cognitive Science Society, 2008, p. 2288.

[12] D. C. Dennett, From Bacteria to Bach and Back: The Evolution of Minds. W W Norton & Co Inc, 2 2018.

[13] M. Kitajima, M. Toyota, and J. Dinet, "How Resonance Works for Development and Propagation of Memes," International Journal on Advances in Systems and Measurements, vol. 14, 2021, pp. 148–161.

[14] M. Kitajima, M. Toyota, and J. Dinet, "Art and Brain with Kazuo Takiguchi," in COGNITIVE 2023 : The Fifteenth International Conference on Advanced Cognitive Technologies and Applications, 2023, pp. 1–10.

[15] K. T. Nakahira, M. Kitajima, and M. Toyota, "Understanding Practice Stages for a Proficient Piano Player to Complete a Piece: Focusing on the Interplay Between Conscious and Unconscious Processes," International Journal on Advances in Life Sciences, vol. 16, 2024, pp. 164–177.

Beyond the Walls: Comparison of Three Extended Reality Technologies Giving Care Home Residents Access to Tourism and Cultural Content for Health and Wellbeing

Hannah Bradwell, Katherine Edwards, Leonie Cooper, Rory Baxter, Arunangsu Chatterjee, Ray B. Jones.
Centre for Heath Technology
University of Plymouth, Plymouth, UK
Email: Hannah.bradwell@plymouth.ac.uk

Catherine Hennessy
Faculty of Social Sciences
University of Stirling
Stirling, Scotland

Abstract— **Previous research into extended reality (XR) technologies for older adults in residential care was limited. We explored use of three XR technologies giving virtual access to a unique UK visitor centre (Eden Project). Three care homes were able to use over three months either (i) Virtual Reality (VR) headsets, (ii) a tablet option or (iii) a projector and screen. While (i) provided fully immersive VR, both (ii, iii) provided augmented reality content. The participants were 22 residents (mean age 86) and 5 staff. Interview and diary data suggested all three XR technologies provided meaningful activities, with enhanced access to nature experiences, increased conversation, reminiscence, calming behavioural escalations and education. Group viewing of the projector was felt beneficial for group interaction and staff resources but was too passive compared to VR or tablet. Some combination of the projector communal experience with the interactivity of VR and tablets is needed. However, in a sector with major workloads and staff shortages, implementation is problematic.**

Keywords- Care homes; extended reality; virtual reality; culture; accessibility.

I. INTRODUCTION

Population demographics are shifting globally due to increased life expectancy, leading to a growing proportion of older adults [1]. This places additional strain on health and social care (H&SC) systems, as aging correlates with declining physical function and increased service demand [2][3]. At the same time, workforce shortages exacerbate these challenges, prompting calls for innovative technologies to support healthy aging [4].

Care homes often present issues like loneliness and lack of stimulation [5], making efforts to improve wellbeing crucial [6]. Extended reality (XR) technologies—encompassing Virtual Reality (VR), Augmented Reality (AR), and mixed reality (MR)—offer immersive and interactive experiences that can promote meaningful activities, social engagement, and access to otherwise inaccessible cultural or heritage sites [7]. Access to culture is linked to health benefits like enhanced quality of life and connectedness [8, 9], but older adults often face barriers in accessing physical heritage sites [10]. The COVID-19 pandemic highlighted the value of virtual access to cultural experiences [11], with VR emerging as a promising tool for older adults, particularly for travel and reminiscence [12][13].

XR interventions may also reduce social isolation, linked to serious health risks, such as cardiovascular diseases [14]. Meaningful activities provided by XR could enhance quality of life and mental health, addressing the connection between physical health and psychological wellbeing [15, 16]. Despite this potential, implementing XR in care homes is challenging, requiring input from staff who mediate technology use [5].

Research on XR in care homes remains limited, with studies identifying usability issues and mixed outcomes for residents with dementia [19]–[21]. Existing literature provides useful insights but often lacks empirical data or direct comparisons of XR methods, such as VR headsets versus AR tablets [18][22]. Understanding the suitability, barriers, and impacts of different XR technologies for care homes is essential for future advancements. This study seeks to address these gaps by exploring the perspectives of both residents and staff, offering feasibility data to guide further research. As such, our aims were as follows. This study evaluated care home residents' experiences with three XR methods for accessing the Eden Project: (i) VR headset, (ii) AR content on a tablet, and (iii) an AR projector with an immersive "room with a view" setup. It also assessed the feasibility of using the WHO-QOL-BREF quality-of-life questionnaire in this context. The study explored user experiences, feasibility, acceptability, device impacts, and barriers during implementation, aiming to compare the three XR approaches and inform future XR design for care home residents.

We first present our methods in section II, including study design, ethical approval, description of sites and participants, materials, procedure, data collection and analysis, followed by results (qualitative, quantitative) in section III, discussion in section IV and finally section V, conclusion.

II. METHODS

Here, we detail methods used for this mixed-methods exploration of XR technologies.

A. Design

A mixed-method exploratory design was used, combining qualitative insights with quantitative measures to balance their respective limitations [23]. Quantitative pre/post measures primarily assessed feasibility, while qualitative data were gathered during and after the study to provide in-depth understanding.

B. Ethics

The study received approval from the University of Plymouth Faculty of Health Ethics Committee. All participants demonstrated capacity to consent and provided written consent after reviewing the participant information.

C. Sites

Three care homes were recruited through collaborators in social care, with no prior involvement in related studies. Participants included five female staff members and 22 residents (average age 86, range 68–97) who completed pre-assessments and interacted with technologies. Thirteen residents and five staff participated in end-of-study interviews or focus groups. Challenges for end-of-study data included closure of one care home, dispersing participants, and two resident deaths, leading to some loss of post-data.

TABLE I. DEMOGRAPHIC DETAILS ON THE CARE HOMES, TECHNOLOGY RECEIVED, PARTICIPANTS, STAFF AND DATA COLLECTED AT EACH SITE.

Care Home	**Technology**	**Care Home Description**
Care Home 1 (CH1)	Individual Tablet Experience	29 bed dementia friendly home, residents with different levels of dementia, residential care needs further to some nursing needs.
Care Home 2 (CH2)	Group Projector Experience	38-bed residential and dementia friendly care home.
Care Home 3 (CH3)	Immersive VR Experience	34-bed dementia friendly residential and nursing home
Care Home	**Pre-study Participants**	**Post-study Participants**
Care Home 1 (CH1)	7 residents (2 male, 5 female)	7 residents (2 m, 5 f) 3 staff focus group (3 f) (2 x activity coordinators, 1 x health care assistant/trainee nurse practitioner) 26 calendar entries
Care Home 2 (CH2)	8 residents (4 male, 4 female)	5 residents (2 m, 3 f) 1 staff interview (1 f) 1 calendar entry
Care Home 3 (CH3)	7 residents (3 male, 4 female)	2 residents (only 1 m interviewed) 1 staff interview (1 f) 0 calendar entries

D. Materials

Each care home was assigned an XR technology. Home 1 received four iPad Pro tablets with optional headphones for exploring Eden Project 360° video content, which included Augmented Reality (AR) overlays, live streams, animations, and interactive maps. Home 2 received an Epson projector and screen for communal AR experiences of Eden Project biomes, navigated via an iPad. Home 3 used two Oculus Quest 2 VR headsets for individual immersive 360° video exploration. All care homes received comparable Eden Project content and a Lenovo tablet for recording staff audio observations.

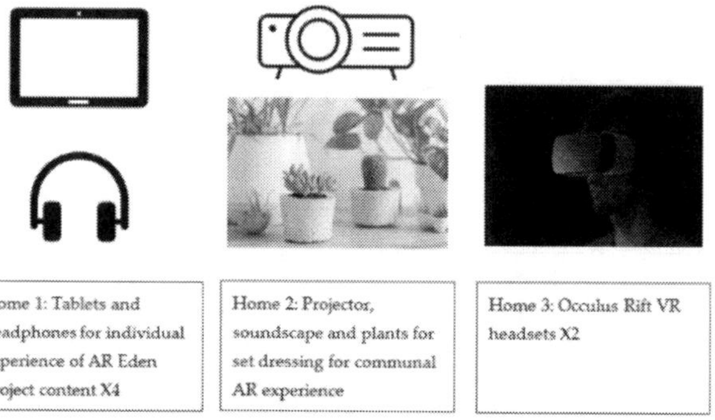

Figure 1. Technology implemented in the care homes

E. The Eden Project content

The Eden Project is a cultural site in Cornwall providing access to the exotic natural world, with large biomes containing one of the world's biggest indoor rainforests and a mediterranean biome. All devices provided curated digital experiences of the Eden Project, including 360° tours of the Rainforest Biome, a Virtual Nature experience, live feeds, and other interactive content. Videos were filmed in sections lasting 4–5 minutes, with an audio guide and ambient soundscapes enhancing immersion.

F. Data collecton

Qualitative data included staff audio observations, end-of-study interviews with residents, and staff focus groups. Quantitative data came from the WHO-QOL-BREF quality-of-life questionnaire, completed at baseline and post-intervention (three months). The short timeframe and small sample size focused on feasibility rather than detecting significant changes.

G. Procedure

Researchers introduced the study to care homes, collected consent, completed baseline measures, and allocated technologies. Home 2 received the projector due to space requirements, while tablets and VR headsets were randomly assigned to Homes 1 and 3. Staff received training on using, maintaining, and collecting data with the devices. Staff encouraged residents to use the technologies twice weekly over three months. Observations were recorded as brief, real-time audio diaries, capturing resident reactions and perceived impacts. This event-based sampling ensured ecological validity [24]. Technology use was left flexible to reflect real-world conditions, with usage rates indicating adoption levels. Post-intervention, researchers repeated the WHO-QOL-BREF assessments and conducted interviews and focus groups with participants before debriefing.

H. *Data analyis*

Audio logs, interviews, and focus groups were transcribed and analyzed using deductive thematic analysis [25]. Three researchers collaboratively coded and validated themes based on evidence, comparing results across XR methods. WHO-QOL-BREF data were scored and analyzed with paired Wilcoxon signed-rank tests to compare pre- and post-intervention scores for each site, excluding assessments with more than 20% missing data [26].

III. RESULTS

We present our results in two sections, focusing on qualitative results first, followed by quantitative results.

A. *Qualitative Results*

TABLE II. THEMES AND INITIAL CODES RESULTING FROM ANALYSIS OF INTERVIEWS AND DIARY ENTRIES (TABLE OF EXAMPLE EVIDENCE AVAILABLE ON REQUEST).

Accessibility to tourism/culture/nature:
Projector allows residents to see new things; Residents enjoyed seeing different environment on VR; Residents felt immersed in nature with VR; Promoting visit to Eden through VR; VR useful for exploring nature; Promoting visit to Eden through tablets; Tablets gave access to culture/outdoors during lockdown and generally for people less active.
Positive outcomes of technology use:
Projector elicited conversation; Residents praise for projector; Social interaction with VR for residents and staff; Residents loved VR experience; Residents enjoyed nature connection experience on VR; Tablet potential for family memories; Residents benefitted from tablets; Tablets provided activity during lockdown and general care home situation; Tablets brought out emotions; Tablets calmed behaviour escalations; Tablets provided entertainment; Tablets provided meaningful activity; Tablets relieve boredom; Tablets prompt reminiscence; Residents enjoyed tablets for being educational impressive and interesting; Residents shared tablet experience with family; Tablets bring back memories; Tablet encouraged social contact and conversation.
Technology appropriateness:
Technologies not suitable (projector home); Residents do not enjoy tablets (VR home); Tablet headphones disliked; Headphones disrupted conversations about tablet; Quick uptake of tablets by residents; Independent use of tablets; Unfamiliar with tablet technology; Tablet bit small for residents to see, icons too small; Residents limited dexterity.
Technology adoption/engagement:
Residents requesting use of projector; Residents would continue projector use; Residents engaged with projector; Staff ease of use of projector; Residents and staff VR easy to use; Residents found VR HMD comfortable; Up to 30 minutes engagement with tablet; Daily tablet use; Future use of tablet desired; Increased tablet use over time; No technology issues with tablet; Tablet easy to learn for staff.
Resource requirement for technology implementation:
Lack of staff time for projector; Staff require training for VR use; VR needed staff support; Limited staff capacity to facilitate tablet use; Staff resources required for tablet use; Residents need help holding tablet; Residents not confident to use tablets alone; Tablet facilitation requires enthusiasm; Tablets require one-to-one facilitation.
Benefits of group technology use:
Residents enjoyed group activity with projector; Tablet group stated shared experience would be easier/more inclusive.
Enjoyed technology features:
Residents enjoyed projector soundscape; Residents enjoyed projector colours; People watching on tablet live feed; Residents enjoyed tablet scenery; Residents enjoyed tablet soundscape; Tablets easily portable to share around practical size.
Technology improvements:
Improvements to projector; Projector content improvements; Desire educational content in VR; Limited attention holding with tablet; Tablet needs more content variety; Tablet had novelty effect.
Implementation issues:
Residents struggled with viewing projector; Projector room lighting difficulties; Require multiple VR headsets; VR did not work in some conditions (lighting); Tablet challenges; Resident tiredness barrier with tablets.
Negative experience/ non-acceptance:
Projector did not meet staff expectations; Projector lack of engagement from residents; Projector use reduced over project period; Projector not stimulating enough; Residents prefer outdoor activity to watching projector; Projector better suited elsewhere; Residents uncomfortable with VR HMD initially; VR disorientating for residents; Some residents found tablet strange; Tablet confusing for some residents

1) *Overview*

The experiences of three care homes using different XR technologies—tablets, VR headsets, and projectors—highlighted the benefits, barriers, and impacts of these technologies for providing remote access to cultural experiences like virtual visits to the Eden Project. Data was gathered from resident (R) and staff interviews (S), as well as diary entries (D), over three months. Table 2 summarizes the key themes and subcodes.

a) *Accessibilty to Tourism, Culture and Nature*

All XR technologies improved accessibility to cultural and natural experiences, with tablets and VR headsets outperforming projectors in creating a sense of presence. VR provided an immersive "360-degree nature" experience, with one resident commenting, "It's like being somewhere else" (CH3, R1). Staff in CH3 noted the benefit of enabling residents to participate despite mobility limitations: "They didn't miss out. They had a part of something" (CH3, S1). Tablets also fostered accessibility, with residents appreciating the beauty of the Eden Project despite the inability to visit in person. For example, one resident stated, "Some of it is absolutely beautiful... I haven't been able to do that for a while" (CH1, R4).

Projectors, while appreciated for communal activities, lacked the immersive and individual engagement provided by tablets and VR. Both VR and tablets inspired interest in real-world visits, expressed by staff and residents.

2) *Positive Outcomes of Technology Use*

The XR technologies produced various positive outcomes:

- Social Interaction: The projector encouraged group discussions, such as safety near water (CH2, S2-D), while tablets facilitated one-on-one conversations, often deepening familial bonds ("She was teaching her daughter"—CH1, S4).
- Reminiscence: Tablets uniquely promoted reminiscence, particularly for residents familiar with the Eden Project. One resident recalled, "I remember visiting with my husband" (CH1, R1).
- Entertainment and Education: Tablets provided entertainment during COVID-19 isolation and were praised for their educational content. Staff noted their calming effect on residents having "bad days" (CH1, S1-D).
- Meaningful Activities: VR was meaningful for gardening enthusiasts, while tablets offered a variety of engaging activities. Staff and residents reported positive emotional responses and a sense of achievement.

3) Technology Appropriateness

Each technology had varying levels of appropriateness based on resident capabilities:

- Tablets: Accessible for able residents but challenging for those with sight or dexterity issues. Staff appreciated their portability but noted the need for guidance.
- VR: Preferred in homes with residents requiring passive experiences but less engaging for group settings.
- Projectors: Most suitable for group activities but limited in fostering individual engagement.

Challenges included small icons on tablets, the weight of devices, and the disruptive nature of headphones. Passive technologies (VR and projectors) were preferred in homes with residents with severe dementia.

4) Technology Adoption and Engagement

All technologies showed good engagement:

- Residents enjoyed the projector's group experience and requested its use (CH2, R3).
- Tablets were used daily but required consistent staff facilitation, which was challenging due to staffing shortages.
- VR was comfortable and easy to operate but primarily offered individual experiences.

Despite these challenges, staff reported an increased willingness to use the technologies over time, highlighting the importance of tailored content for sustained interest.

5) Resource Requirments

Implementing XR technologies required significant staff input:

- Tablets necessitated one-on-one interaction, limiting scalability in larger groups.
- VR and projectors were easier to operate but still required staff training and facilitation.
- Staffing shortages due to COVID-19 exacerbated these challenges, with staff balancing care duties and technology use.

6) Group Technology Use and Enjoyment

Residents favored group activities facilitated by projectors, with staff in tablet-equipped homes suggesting larger screens for communal use. Nature content, live streams, and soundscapes were universally praised. The portability of tablets was noted as a key advantage for individualised experiences.

7) Technology Improvements

To sustain engagement, all technologies would benefit from updated content and user-friendly interfaces. Suggestions included more immersive features for projectors and larger icons for tablets. Staff emphasized the need for resources to support ongoing technology use, including training and additional staff capacity.

Overall, each XR technology offered unique benefits and challenges. Tablets were versatile and engaging but required staff support. VR provided immersive, individual experiences, while projectors facilitated group activities. Tailoring technologies to resident capabilities and care home contexts is crucial for maximizing their impact.

TABLE III. SUMMARY OF BENEFITS AND LIMITATIONS OF EACH TECHNOLOGY.

XR Technology Type	Benefits	Limitations
Across all three technologies	Allowed residents to see new things Access to culture, nature, heritage experiences Meaningful activity, entertainment Improve resident behaviour and mood Tool to aid reminiscence Nature sounds	Poor resident eyesight impacts use of all technologies All require more variety of content for longer term engagement Could include more educational content New technologies can be confusing initially
VR	Immersive experience in new environments Individual experience 'Passive' activity for those with advanced dementia and/or reduced capacity Doesn't require large physical space for use	High levels of staff input needed to facilitate use Training need for staff Challenging for use in communal environments Image quality sensitive to daylight Headset discomfort Disorientation in headset
AR Tablet	Promoted interest in real world visits to Eden Good engagement and emotional response Created access to culture/outdoors during lockdown for those less active Mediated conversation Provided educational activity Easy to use for most Convenient for portability Doesn't require large physical space for use	Difficulty for those with limited dexterity Required a level of capacity for interaction Headphone use not enjoyable for residents Headphone use limited social interaction High levels of staff input needed to facilitate use Heavy to hold Challenging for use in communal environments as individual activity Residents found initial use challenging Small icons hard to see
AR Projector	Promoted social conversation more than	Perceived as less immersive access to culture and nature

	other technologies 'Passive' activity for those with more advance dementia and/or reduced capacity Group activity Requires less staff resource to facilitate than individual technologies	than tablet and VR Required staff resources to set up and use Sunlight disrupted image quality Activity was too passive Required large physical space for use Too passive less engaging

B. *Quantitative Results*

WHO quality of life pre-study data was collected for 22 residents, while post-study data was only collected from 14 residents. The closure of Home 3 had a significant impact on the post-study data collection. There were additionally two participants lost to study (deceased) in the Projector home and one who was unavailable for data collection at the time of researchers visit.

TABLE IV. MEAN WHO-QOL-BREF SCORES PRE AND POST TECHNOLOGY USE PERIOD.

		Quality of Life		Satisfaction with Health		Physical Health	
Group (N)	Tech	Pre	Post	Pre	Post	Pre	Post
Home 1 (N=7 pre, 2 post)	Tablet	4.1	3.7	4.1	3.6	66	63
Home 2 (N= 7 pre, 7 post)	Projector	4.1	3.8	3.5	2.8	54	59
Home 3 (N= 8 pre, 5 post)	VR	2.9	3.0	3.4	3.5	54	46
		Psychological Health		**Social Relationships**		**Environmental Health**	
Group (N)	Tech	Pre	Post	Pre	Post	Pre	Post
Home 1 (N=7 pre, 2 post)	Tablet	59	67	39	52	66	74
Home 2 (N= 7 pre, 7 post)	Projector	60	68	58	67	77	73
Home 3 (N= 8 pre, 5 post)	VR	52	50	37	58	61	47

The WHO-QOL-BREF was administered pre- and post-technology implementation at each site. Mean scores for each category were calculated and are shown in Table 4. Researchers found the WHO-QOL-BREF too lengthy for older adult care home residents, particularly for larger samples, as participants often reported fatigue and dissatisfaction with the time required. Some questions were deemed irrelevant or overly personal. Given these limitations—the feasibility of this measure for future studies with larger samples and longer time-frames is deemed limited.

IV. DISCUSSION

This study compared three XR technologies (VR, AR tablet, AR projector) in care homes, relying primarily on qualitative data and exploring the feasibility of the WHO-QOL-BREF measure in this context. While prior research has explored XR implementations in care settings [5][18][19][22], this is the first study to compare different XR types, providing valuable insights for future technology design, development, and implementation in care homes.

All three XR technologies demonstrated strong potential for care home use, aligning with earlier findings [13][18]. Engagement levels varied, with the tablet praised for its interactive design, which encouraged active participation and elicited positive emotional responses. In contrast, the projector, as a more passive medium, was seen as less engaging for residents who could actively interact with content but was noted as more suitable for those with severe dementia. The VR headset offered immersive experiences but presented challenges, such as physical discomfort, consistent with previous concerns regarding head-mounted displays for older adults [18][21]. These findings highlight the need for further exploration of technology-specific dynamics in care settings.

The XR technologies facilitated virtual access to cultural and natural environments, which aligns with documented health and wellbeing benefits [9]. Tablets and VR were particularly effective in enhancing inclusivity and providing meaningful engagement, with tablets also noted for reducing behavioral escalation and improving mood. Social interaction was positively impacted across all technologies, with projectors fostering group discussions, and tablets and VR supporting one-on-one interactions with staff and family. The capacity of XR technologies to trigger positive reminiscence further underscores their potential, although prior findings [20] suggest that the possibility of negative reminiscence triggers warrants further investigation.

Practical challenges included the space requirements for projectors and usability barriers with tablets, such as small icons, which posed difficulties for residents with reduced dexterity or eyesight. VR headsets caused physical discomfort and may be unsuitable for residents with dementia, aligning with previous findings [18][21]. Staff facilitation was critical across all XR technologies, with projectors requiring less staff involvement due to their group activity format.

The WHO-QOL-BREF measure proved burdensome and lengthy for this demographic, with residents reporting fatigue and discomfort during completion. Although all participants completed the measure, its relevance and feasibility for care home residents were limited. Shorter, more targeted measures focusing on social interaction, connection to place, and wellbeing would better suit future research. Qualitative methods, particularly audio diaries, were effective in capturing nuanced insights and should be prioritized in similar studies.

V. CONCLUSION

XR technologies hold significant promise in care homes, offering meaningful activities, fostering inclusivity, and providing access to culturally and naturally significant environments. Among the technologies studied, tablets emerged as the most suitable, balancing high engagement with usability, and avoiding the discomfort associated with VR headsets or the passivity of projectors. However, the preference for group activities within care homes, due to communal dynamics and limited staff resources, highlights the need for future XR developments to combine interactivity with communal usability. This is a key area for future research investigation.

ACKNOWLEDGMENT

The Generating Older Active Lives Digitally (GOALD) project was funded by UKRI via the Healthy Ageing Social Behavioural and Design Research Programme (SBDRP), from the Economic and Social Research Council (ESRC) grant number: ES/V016113/1. The EPIC (eHealth Productivity and Innovation in Cornwall and the Isle of Scilly) project was part funded by the European Regional Development Fund. Additional funding for the EPIC project was received from University of Plymouth. ERDF Grant number [05R18P02814]. The ICONIC project (Intergenerational Co-design of Novel Technologies In Coastal Communities) was awarded funding (March 2022) from UKRI/EPSRC grant reference Intergenerational Technology Co-Design Process 25 EP/W024357/1.

We would also like to thank our collaborating care homes, staff, residents and other health care professionals. On behalf of the GOALD project: Catherine H. Hennessy, Faculty of Social Sciences, University of Stirling; Ray B. Jones, Faculty of Health, University of Plymouth; Richard Haynes, Faculty of Arts & Humanities, University of Stirling; Anna C. Whittaker, Faculty of Health Sciences & Sport, University of Stirling (Core Management Team); Sheena Asthana, Plymouth Institute for Health and Care Research (PIHR), University of Plymouth; Rory Baxter, Faculty of Health, University of Plymouth; Hannah Bradwell, Faculty of Health, University of Plymouth; Arunangsu Chatterjee, Faculty of Medicine and Health, University of Leeds; Pete Coffee, School of Social Sciences, Heriot-Watt University; Leonie Cooper, Faculty of Health, University of Plymouth; Alison Dawson, Faculty of Social Sciences, University of Stirling; Katie Edwards, Faculty of Health, University of Plymouth; Swen Gaudl, Faculty of Science & Engineering, University of Plymouth; Tanja Krizaj, Faculty of Health, University of Plymouth; Gregory Mannion, Faculty of Social Sciences, University of Stirling; Gemma Ryde, Institute of Cardiovascular and Medical Sciences, University of Glasgow; Alejandro Veliz Reyes, Faculty of Arts, Humanities and Business, University of Plymouth; John Ritchie, Faculty of Arts & Humanities, University of Stirling; Simone Tomaz, Faculty of Health Sciences & Sport, University of Stirling; Alison Warren, Faculty of Health, University of Plymouth; Karen Watchman, Faculty of Health Sciences & Sport, University of Stirling; Katherine Willis, Faculty of Arts, Humanities and Business, University of Plymouth, and partners—Active Stirling Ltd., Generations Working Together, Hearing Loss Cornwall, Nudge Community Builders, South Asian Society (Devon and Cornwall), Sporting Heritage, Sports Heritage Scotland, St. Breward Community, iSightCornwall, UKActive. We would also like to acknowledge our thanks to the Eden Project for their collaboration on this study.

Institutional Review Board Statement: This study was reviewed and approved by the University of Plymouth Faculty of Health Ethics Committee (code: 2773), approval date 05/07/2021. All participants had capacity to consent and provided written consent following confirming their understanding of the provided participant information.

Author Contributions: Conceptualization, H.B., K.E., L.C., and R.B.; methodology, H.B., K.E., L.C., and R.B; data collection, H.B., K.E., L.C., and R.B, data analysis, H.B., K.E., L.C., and R.B.; writing—original draft preparation, H.B.; writing—review and editing, H.B., K.E., L.C., R.B., A.C. C.H., and R.J.; project administration,, A.C., C.H. and R.J.; funding acquisition, A.C., C.H., and R.J.. All authors have read and agreed to the published version of the manuscript.

REFERENCES

[1] J. Abdi, A. Al-Hindawi, T. Ng, and M. P. Vizcaychipi. "Scoping review on the use of socially assistive robot technology in elderly care." BMJ Open, vol 8, no 2, pp 18815, 2018. DOI:https://doi.org/10.1136/bmjopen-2017-018815

[2] W. Moyle, C. Jones, L. Pu, and S-C. Chen. "Applying user-centred research design and evidence to develop and guide the use of technologies, including robots, in aged care." Contemporary Nurse, vol 54, no 1, pp 1–3, 2018. DOI:http://dx.doi.org/10.1080/10376178.2017.1438057

[3] L. Garçon et al. Medical and Assistive Health Technology: Meeting the needs of aging populations." The Gerontologist, vol 56, Suppl 2, 2016. DOI:http://dx.doi.org/10.1093/geront/gnw005

[4] UK Parliament. "Robotics in Social Care. Houses of Parliament Post Note." from https://post.parliament.uk/research-briefings/post-pn-0591/ [retrieved: October, 2024]

[5] J. Waycott, et al. "The role of staff in facilitating immersive virtual reality for enrichment in aged care: An ethic of Care Perspective." CHI Conference on Human Factors in Computing Systems, 2022. DOI:http://dx.doi.org/10.1145/3491102.3501956

[6] M. T. Siniscarco, C. Love-Williams, and S. Burnett-Wolle. "Video conferencing: An intervention for emotional loneliness in long-term care." Activities, Adaptation & Aging, vol 41, no 4, pp 316–329, 2017. DOI:http://dx.doi.org/10.1080/01924788.2017.1326763

[7] S.S.Y. Wang. "Use of Extended Reality in Medicine During the COVID-19 Pandemic." In: A. S. Pillai, G. Guazzaroni, (eds) Extended Reality Usage During COVID 19 Pandemic. Intelligent Systems Reference Library, vol 216. Springer, Cham. 2022. https://doi.org/10.1007/978-3-030-91394-6_1

[8] Unesco. "Right to participate in cultural life." Unesco. 2021. from https://en.unesco.org/human-rights/cultural-life [retrieved: October, 2024].

[9] The Heritage Alliance. "Heritage Alliance Annual Report." from https://www.theheritagealliance.org.uk/wp-content/uploads/2020/10/Heritage-Alliance-AnnualReport_2020_Online.pdf [retrieved: October, 2024]

[10] A. Marasco and B. Balbi. "Designing accessible experiences for heritage visitors through virtual reality." from https://ertr-ojs-tamu.tdl.org/ertr/article/view/526 [retrieved: September, 2024]

[11] E. Kużelewska and M. Tomaszuk. "European Human Rights Dimension of the online access to cultural heritage in times of the COVID-19 Outbreak." International Journal for the Semiotics of Law, vol 35, no 3, pp 1067–1079, 2020. DOI:http://dx.doi.org/10.1007/s11196-020-09712-x

[12] A. Paladini et al. "Impact of virtual reality experience on accessibility of Cultural Heritage." The International Archives of the Photogrammetry, Remote Sensing and Spatial Information Sciences, vol XLII-2/W11, pp 929–936, 2019. DOI:http://dx.doi.org/10.5194/isprs-archives-xlii-2-w11-929-2019

[13] K. S. Thach, R. Lederman, and J. Waycott. "How older adults respond to the use of Virtual Reality for enrichment: a systematic review." In 32nd Australian Conference on Human-Computer Interaction (OzCHI '20), December 02–04, 2020, Sydney, NSW, Australia. ACM, New York, NY, USA, 11 pages. https://doi.org/10.1145/3441000.3441003

[14] Campaign to End Loneliness. (N.D). "Facts and statistics, Campaign to End Loneliness." Available at: https://www.campaigntoendloneliness.org/facts-and-statistics/ [retrieved: September, 2024]

[15] N. Smith, A-M. Towers, S. Palmer, J. Beecham & E. Welch. "Being occupied: Supporting 'meaningful activity' in care homes for older people in England." Ageing & Society, vol 38, no 11, pp 2218-2240, 2018. doi:10.1017/S0144686X17000678

[16] A. Steptoe, A. Deaton, and A. A. Stone. "Subjective wellbeing, health, and ageing." The Lancet, vol 385, no 9968, pp 640–648, 2015. DOI:http://dx.doi.org/10.1016/s0140-6736(13)61489-0

[17] Age UK. "Later Life in the United Kingdom." from https://www.ageuk.org.uk/globalassets/age-uk/documents/reports-and-publications/later_life_uk_factsheet.pdf [retrieved: October, 2024]

[18] A. V. Vanden et al. "Immersive Virtual Reality for Older Adults: Empirically Grounded Design Guidelines." ACM Trans. Access. Comput. vol 14, no 3, Article 14, 30 pages, 2021. https://doi.org/10.1145/3470743

[19] E. A. M. Abels et al. "Augmented reality-based remote family visits in nursing homes." ACM International Conference on Interactive Media Experiences, 2021. DOI:http://dx.doi.org/10.1145/3452918.3465502

[20] M. Sultana et al. "Virtual reality experience intervention may reduce responsive behaviors in nursing home residents with dementia: A case series." Journal of Alzheimer's Disease, vol 84, no 2, pp 883–893, 2021. DOI:http://dx.doi.org/10.3233/jad-210010

[21] S. Baker, et al, "Evaluating the use of interactive virtual reality technology with older adults living in residential aged care." Information Processing & Management, vol 57, no 3, 2020, https://doi.org/10.1016/j.ipm.2019.102105.

[22] J-H. Kim, S. Park, and H. Lim. "Developing a virtual reality for people with dementia in nursing homes based on their psychological needs: A feasibility study." BMC Geriatrics, vol 21, no 1, 2021. DOI:http://dx.doi.org/10.1186/s12877-021-02125-w

[23] J. M. Azorín and R. Cameron. 2010. "The application of mixed methods in organisational research: A literature review." Journal of Business Research Methods, vol 8, no 2, pp 95-105, 2010.

[24] T. Lischetzke, T. Könen. "Daily Diary Methodology." In: F. Maggino, (eds) Encyclopedia of Quality of Life and Well-Being Research. Springer, Cham. 2021 https://doi.org/10.1007/978-3-319-69909-7_657-2

[25] V. Braun and V. Clarke. "Thematic analysis." In Liamputtong P. (Ed.). Handbook of Research Methods in Health Social Sciences. Springer, Singapore, 2019.

[26] World Health Organization.. "Programme on mental health: WHOQOL user manual, 2012 revision." World Health Organization. from: https://apps.who.int/iris/handle/10665/77932 [retrieved: October, 2024]

Enhancing School Visits to Museums through Gamified VR: A Complementary Approach to Learning and Social Engagement

Cleiton Pons Ferreira
Research and Innovation Department
Federal Institute of Education, Science and Technology of Rio Grande do Sul
Rio Grande, Brazil
e-mail: cleiton.ferreira@riogrande.ifrs.edu.br

Paula Latorre; Francisco Antonio Nieto-Escamez
CIBIS Research Center
University of Almeria
Almeria, Spain
e-mail: plr791@ual.es , pnieto@ual.es

Abstract— **Science education faces challenges in engaging students, especially when abstract concepts lack tangible representation. Museums bridge this gap by blending theory with hands-on exploration, but guided tours often remain passive. To increase engagement, this paper presents a hybrid methodology that integrates Gamified Virtual Reality (GVR) with museum experiences. Originally designed to be implemented at the Natural History Pavilion of the University of Almería, the proposed activities, such as "The Intruder" and "Minerals in My Life," encourage students to interact with exhibits through immersive and collaborative tasks. This approach promotes both scientific literacy and social-emotional skills. Although there are technical and financial constraints, partnerships and affordable VR solutions can mitigate these challenges. Future research should explore the long-term impact of this model on interdisciplinary learning.**

Keywords- Virtual Reality; Gamification; Science Museums; Education; Interactive Learning.

I. INTRODUCTION

Science education is essential to develop critical thinking and understanding of the real world, preparing students for life and the challenges of society. However, when addressing these aspects, traditional teaching methods, often centered on lectures and memorization, fail to engage students, especially when faced with abstract and difficult-to-understand concepts [1]. This disconnect is exacerbated in contexts where the lack of practical resources limits the ability to transform theories into tangible experiences, reinforcing the need for innovative approaches.

Science museums, recognized as informal learning spaces, provide a bridge between theory and practice through interactive exhibits [2]. However, even in these environments, many guided tours perpetuate a passive model in which students assume the role of observers, without actively interacting with the content or establishing meaningful connections between the concepts presented and their real-world applications. This limitation underutilizes the educational potential of museums, which could serve as living laboratories for scientific exploration.

The GVR emerges as a response to these challenges, transforming static observation into an immersive and collaborative experience [3]. For example, by exploring digital habitats or identifying minerals in everyday virtual environments, students not only assimilate scientific knowledge but also develop metacognitive skills, such as problem-solving and decision-making. This approach resonates with contemporary demands for Science, Technology, Engineering, and Mathematics (STEM) education that prioritizes digital literacy and prepares students for an increasingly technological world [4].

Furthermore, gamification incorporates playful elements—such as missions, rewards, and healthy competitions—that enhance intrinsic motivation and engagement. When combined with VR, this strategy not only facilitates the assimilation of complex content, but also promotes socio-emotional skills, such as communication and collaboration, which are essential for the student's comprehensive education [5]. By adopting these technologies, museums transcend their traditional role as repositories of knowledge, becoming dynamic spaces where learning is collectively constructed, and not just transmitted. This transformation, however, does not occur without obstacles. The effectiveness of GVR depends on careful pedagogical design, which avoids prioritizing technical aspects to the detriment of clear educational objectives. Furthermore, new technological tools to support education cannot focus on merely virtual and individualistic learning, since access to available physical resources and interaction with peers throughout the learning process are also essential. Therefore, aligned with the needs of students and the principles of experiential learning, this proposed methodology represents a significant advance in the way we conceive the relationship between education, technology and social engagement.

The paper is structured as follows. In Section II, the state of the art on VR and gamification in museums is presented. In Section III, the hybrid methodology and the respective proposed activities are detailed. In Section IV, the benefits, challenges and expected outcomes are discussed. Finally, conclusions and future directions are addressed in Section V.

II. STATE OF THE ART ON VR AND GAMIFICATION IN MUSEUMS

The integration of VR into museum experiences has gained significant attention in recent years. Studies highlight its potential to transform traditional museum visits by increasing interactivity and engagement through immersive digital environments [6],[7]. Research in this domain typically focuses on leveraging VR to enhance individual learning experiences, allowing visitors to explore historical reconstructions, scientific simulations, and cultural heritage artifacts in new ways [8]. Gamification can further enhance these experiences by incorporating elements such as challenges, rewards, and collaborative quests, effectively increasing motivation and knowledge retention [9]. Several studies show that combining VR with gamified strategies promotes cognitive and socio-emotional gains [10], [11]. Despite these advances, the application of hybrid VR models that integrate physical and digital museum visits remains underexplored. Most studies on this topic emphasize fully immersive digital content or augmented on-site enhancements without a connection between the real and virtual environments [8]. A crucial gap in current research is the lack of strategies that facilitate social and cooperative learning in VR-enhanced museum environments. Although collaborative VR applications exist in other educational contexts, their adaptation to school group visits remains minimal, limiting their potential to support teamwork, communication, and collective problem-solving [9]. This study addresses these limitations by proposing a model that merges physical museum visits with collaborative GVR tasks. Unlike previous approaches, the methodology proposed in this paper offers active and collaborative participation to solve educational challenges, demonstrating the potential of structured hybrid VR models to enrich science education beyond traditional classroom settings.

III. METHODOLOGY

The proposed hybrid methodology was developed in response to the demand for virtual reality experimentation with school-age children, integrating both physical and virtual visits to the Natural History Pavilion at the University of Almería. The concept was designed around two GVR activities:

- The Intruder: After physically visiting the museum's display cases, which showcase different plant and animal habitats, students use VR headsets to explore the same environments, now virtually modified. Their task is to identify misplaced species by comparing them to the physical specimens previously observed. Meanwhile, classmates actively participate in resolving discrepancies between the virtual and real displays.
- Minerals in My Life: Similar to the previous activity, students first visit the museum's collection of stones and minerals, learning about their primary applications in daily life. They then explore VR-based residential and workplace environments featuring commercial products and equipment that incorporate minerals as raw materials. The gamified activity, conducted collaboratively with peers, involves identifying the minerals present in various everyday objects within the virtual environments.

The design of the these idealized activity models is based on collaborative VR structures and gamification strategies that have been shown to enhance engagement [10] and improve the contextualization of scientific concepts through situated learning [11]. Beyond the museum's physical resources, implementing the gamified activity requires a 360° camera for capturing the images, a platform for creating a virtual tour, and VR headsets. Additionally, the creation of pre- and post-activity assessments is essential for evaluating conceptual understanding and teamwork, aligning these evaluations with cognitive and socio-emotional assessments while also providing feedback for refining the model.

IV. BENEFITS, CHALLENGES AND EXPECTED OUTCOMES

The proposed hybrid methodology offers substantial advantages for science education. By integrating collaborative VR tasks into museum visits, students transition from passive observers to active participants in dynamic problem-solving scenarios that mirror real-world scientific challenges. The immersive nature of VR enhances intrinsic motivation, as gamified activities are perceived as inherently engaging and rewarding. This leads to greater student involvement and improved knowledge retention compared to traditional observation-based learning. Additionally, the interactive design fosters peer-to-peer learning, enabling students to exchange ideas, critique hypotheses, and refine solutions through discussion, thereby strengthening both cognitive and social skills.

Despite these benefits, the implementation of this approach presents several practical and pedagogical challenges. One major obstacle is financial: high-quality VR hardware can be cost-prohibitive for institutions with limited budgets. While low-cost alternatives, such as smartphone-based VR viewers, offer a potential solution, their impact on immersion and interactivity must be carefully assessed. Moreover, sustaining these initiatives requires strong institutional partnerships. Without such collaborations, scalability remains a significant hurdle, particularly for smaller institutions. Another critical concern lies in the design of the gamification itself. If not carefully structured, gamified elements risk reducing learning to a superficial competition for points or badges rather than fostering deep educational engagement. Addressing these challenges demands meticulous planning, continuous teacher training, and iterative feedback mechanisms to fine-tune the balance between engagement and educational rigor while optimizing the relationship between real and virtual learning.

The implementation of the proposed hybrid methodology is expected to yield several positive outcomes. First, it aims to enhance student engagement by transforming conventional museum visits into interactive and participatory learning experiences. By incorporating VR-based gamified tasks, students are likely to exhibit higher motivation and improved retention of scientific concepts, as previous research indicates that immersive learning environments facilitate deeper cognitive processing. Furthermore, this approach is expected to promote collaborative problem-solving skills, as students work together to complete tasks and explore real-world applications of science. Another anticipated outcome is the development of socio-emotional competencies, including communication and teamwork, as peer interaction plays a fundamental role in the learning process. Finally, this methodology has the potential to serve as a scalable model for other educational institutions, paving the way for further research into the long-term impact of GVR in science education.

V. CONCLUSIONS AND FUTURE DIRECTIONS

This study introduced a hybrid methodology that integrates GVR into museum experiences, aiming to transform traditional visits for student groups into immersive and participatory activities. To this end, practical activities were designed based on principles of gamification, situated learning, and collaborative participation, utilizing resources such as physical visits, 360° VR, and pre- and post-activity assessments as feedback mechanisms to refine the methodological design. The approach promotes active engagement, integrates theoretical knowledge with practical applications in a playful way. Collaborative tasks in VR, when integrated into the physical environment, not only facilitate the retention of complex scientific concepts but also enhance socio-emotional skills, such as communication and teamwork. As museums evolve into dynamic and interdisciplinary centers, it is crucial not only to adopt technological innovations but also to implement them within contexts that foster meaningful learning for comprehensive and inclusive education, thus exploring the full potential of these simulation tools.

For future guidance, it is recommended to investigate the long-term impact of this methodology as an interdisciplinary resource and promoter of skills and competencies. Comparative studies across different age groups and socioeconomic contexts could enhance the inclusiveness of the model. Additionally, it is essential to explore the integration of artificial intelligence and sensors such as eye tracking in VR to personalize experiences and improve real-time feedback. Finally, expanding the model to other exhibition spaces related to art, science, and history could consolidate the role of museums and galleries as dynamic environments for pedagogical innovation, aligning them with the advancements in VR and the growing emphasis on creating immersive worlds for education and culture.

ACKNOWLEDGMENT

The authors would like to thank the Federal Institute of Education, Science and Technology of Rio Grande do Sul and the University of Almeria for the support provided.

REFERENCES

[1] V. W. Vongkulluksn, L. Lu, M. J. Nelson, and K. Xie, "Cognitive engagement with technology scale: a validation study", *Educ. Technol. Res. Dev.*, vol. 70, nº 2, pp. 419–445, apr. 2022, doi: 10.1007/s11423-022-10098-9.

[2] E. H. S. Chng and T. T. M. Tan, "Informal Learning of Science at Science Centers and Museums: Perspectives, Influences, and Issues", in *A Diversity of Pathways Through Science Education*, Y. S. Ong, T. T. M. Tan, and Y.-J. Lee, Orgs., Singapore: Springer Nature Singapore, 2024, pp. 219–244. doi: 10.1007/978-981-97-2607-3_13.

[3] J. Radianti, T. A. Majchrzak, J. Fromm, and I. Wohlgenannt, "A systematic review of immersive virtual reality applications for higher education: Design elements, lessons learned, and research agenda", *Comput. Educ.*, vol. 147, pp. 103778, apr. 2020, doi: 10.1016/j.compedu.2019.103778.

[4] International Commission on the Futures of Education, *Reimagining our futures together: a new social contract for education*. UNESCO, 2021. doi: 10.54675/ASRB4722.

[5] D. Wang and X. Huang, "Transforming education through artificial intelligence and immersive technologies: enhancing learning experiences", *Interact. Learn. Environ.*, pp. 1–20, feb. 2025, doi: 10.1080/10494820.2025.2465451.

[6] Siqi Wang, "Enhancing Art Education Through Virtual Reality: The Impact of Virtual Art Museums on Junior High School Students", *Res. Adv. Educ.*, vol. 3, nº 9, pp. 52–58, sept. 2024, Accessed: 20 March 2025 [Online]. Available in: https://www.paradigmpress.org/rae/article/view/1305

[7] Y. Zhou, J. Chen and M. Wang, "A meta-analytic review on incorporating virtual and augmented reality in museum learning", *Educ. Res. Rev.*, vol. 36, pp. 100454, jun. 2022, doi: 10.1016/j.edurev.2022.100454.

[8] P. P. Yang, W. Schmidt, and D. Vlachopoulos, "Virtual Reality (VR) in Museum Education: A Systematic Literature Review" 14th International Technology, Education and Development Conference, Valencia, Spain, mar. 2020, pp. 4397–4405. doi: 10.21125/inted.2020.1218.

[9] M. K. Bekele, E. Champion, D. A. McMeekin, and H. Rahaman, "The Influence of Collaborative and Multi-Modal Mixed Reality: Cultural Learning in Virtual Heritage", *Multimodal Technol. Interact.*, vol. 5, nº 12, pp. 79, dez. 2021, doi: 10.3390/mti5120079.

[10] M. Portuguez-Castro and H. Santos Garduño, "Beyond Traditional Classrooms: Comparing Virtual Reality Applications and Their Influence on Students' Motivation", *Educ. Sci.*, vol. 14, nº 9, pp. 963, sept. 2024, doi: 10.3390/educsci14090963.

[11] T. Zhuang, X. Xu, and Y. Zhang, "Contextualizing and visualizing abstract theoretical knowledge for situated learning: large-scale VR-supported higher education in China", *Virtual Real.*, vol. 29, nº 1, pp. 4, nov. 2024, doi: 10.1007/s10055-024-01075-z.